Coping with
Bereavement

Other self-help books published by Oneworld:

Coping with Bereavement

Hamish McIlwraith

ONEWORLD

OXFORD

COPING WITH BEREAVEMENT

Oneworld Publications
(Sales and Editorial)
185 Banbury Road
Oxford OX2 7AR
England

Oneworld Publications
(U.S. Marketing Office)
PO Box 830, 21 Broadway
Rockport, MA 01966
U.S.A.

ISBN 1–85168–153–1

Cover design by Design Deluxe
Printed by WSOY, Finland

Contents

Introduction

Death is inevitable. But typically most people avoid the subject until they experience the death of someone close to them. If they do think of death, it's often in terms of how it affects other people. Perhaps avoidance is a mechanism we need in order to function effectively in a world where the reality of wars, accidents, famine and sickness brings an end to life. And to think too closely about death might mean not taking everyday risks such as crossing the road, taking a lift or flying in an aircraft. This 'thoughtlessness' helps us cope.

However, there is an antithesis in not allowing death to invade too closely in our thoughts. In denying death, we tend to deny that it can take *anyone* at *any time*, and through *any* agent or medium. So, when it comes (as it surely will) we can be taken by surprise.

Even then, acknowledging the *fact* of death is not enough. Death isn't just someone being there one day and not being there the next. People who suffer the profound anguish of bereavement not only feel the loss of an individual, but often the ruin of the totality of their whole lives. It's an intense and desperate crisis that devastates individuals and families. Some feel that they simply cannot continue. This is a book that aims to address this sense of hopelessness by providing practical help and advice, and to show

1

that it *is* possible to carry on after someone has died, and re-establish a meaningful life.

This is difficult to do because everyone has a different experience of death. In my own case, death was shocking and unexpected. My wife, Shirin, died in hospital after a short and seemingly minor illness. The last words she ever said to me were: 'Don't be upset.' A few moments later she arrested. She was transferred from her ward to the Intensive Care Unit and despite all the efforts of the medical staff was pronounced dead about an hour later. She was thirty-nine. We had been married for almost seven years.

No-one knows why she died. The consultant treating her was unable to provide a diagnosis, and despite exhaustive investigations by scientists in the Public Health Bureau, all tests proved negative.

I was totally unprepared. Like many people, I'd never thought deeply about the certainty of my own death and did not think that my wife would die so young and without warning. And, of course, when she died I was *very* upset. I experienced an agony of intense, raw pain for weeks afterwards that was physical as well as emotional. But, in the months that followed, I learnt to draw on reserves of strength that anyone who has not experienced the loss of a close relative, but perhaps especially a partner or child, would find difficult to comprehend.

If, like me, you've lost a partner in young adulthood, it is more likely that you will have had little experience of death as compared to someone who has been widowed later in life. For the most part, death for young adults is unexpected. Most of them probably give little thought to the possibility of the death of their partner other than an occasional: 'What if . . . ?' For this reason, they are more likely to find it difficult to adjust to the death of someone close to them than older people, who have been exposed to more experiences of death and have had more time to anticipate and prepare for the death of their partner and of their friends. Young adults tend to personalize death.

In other sad circumstances, children die. Parents often feel that they are somehow responsible. They feel guilt, thinking that they have been remiss in not providing a safe environment for their child. These feelings of failure may be intensified if the child died through miscarriage, stillbirth or cot death. The death of a young child can bring about great strains in a family. Partners often find their relationship less fulfilling than before, and disappointment, bitterness and resentment can follow. They may find it difficult to talk to each other, or with remaining children, which builds barriers to healing.

Most people, however, experience the death of a parent while they themselves are in middle age. Although this does not usually involve the same shock at the seeming senselessness of a younger person's death, adjustments nevertheless need to be made. For example, bereaved offspring who are middle-aged often start to seriously consider the certainty of their own death and begin to 'wind down' their affairs in preparation for it by drawing up a will or discarding physical and emotional clutter from their lives. In addition, many have the shocking realization that there is no-one left in the world who will give them the unconditional love that their parents did.

But, reactions to death are intensely personal and variable. It's probably true to say that while we can empathize, no-one can *really* understand the depth of the emotional turmoil of each individual who has been bereaved. However, it *is* possible to construct a framework for a recovery from the trauma of death that can be applied to most people's circumstances. That is what this book is about.

section one
Death and the Grieving Process

Recently, it seems to have become more difficult for people in Western society to grieve, and to accept death and bereavement. This is probably due to the changing mores concerning death that have occurred during the twentieth century. For example, it is now not always necessary for people to wear black at a funeral or for a minister to give an address in a church. And more elaborate and formal expressions of condolence – such as the wearing of a black armband – are largely no longer observed. Despite the loss of these cultural supports, people who have recently been bereaved are nonetheless expected to cope. Often they are expected to show their grief for only a very short time, despite evidence to suggest that it can take much more than a year for a bereaved person to start to reconstruct their life. This apparent lack of sympathy may be because people tend to confuse *grief*, which is the period of readjustment that a bereaved person needs in order to respond to death (or, perhaps less coldly expressed, the period during which their love is not able to let go), and *mourning*, which is the short period of time during which we make a social acknowledgement that the person we love has died. The period of mourning in modern society is relatively short and is more or less over within a few days or weeks of the funeral.

However, where grieving is concerned, the length of time and the intensity of the period are fairly unpredictable. They depend on your personality, how close you were to the person who died, the previous experiences you've had of death and the way in which your loved one died. Following the sudden death of my wife Shirin, I was told by a friend of a friend, whose husband had died after eleven months of marriage, that it was six months before she found she was able to start to laugh again at the trivia of everyday life. But she didn't tell me that it was going to be a year before I would be able to control bursting into tears at any time of day, or in any place, whether cooking a meal for myself, sitting in my car at a set of traffic lights, or working on a text for a lecture. For some, it can take years.

one

Stages of grief

Despite these differences between individuals' experiences, there seem to be a number of stages and emotions in the grieving process that are common, and which mix and merge from day to day, and even moment to moment. The stages are sometimes presented as an *impact* stage, a *recoil* stage, and finally a *readjustment* stage, but other models concentrate on the wide range of emotions of grief to build up a composite picture of grief. These include: shock, denial, anger, guilt, relief, sadness, despair, anxiety, and, eventually, readjustment built on acceptance and strength drawn from the memories of the good times you had with your loved one.

It has been suggested that this 'logical' ordering of stages and emotions is superficial. This is probably the case. Reactions to death are not straightforward, and appear to involve a waxing and waning of all of these different states and emotions in a roller-coaster interplay of bewilderment and pain. Nevertheless, they are convenient labels which are useful in describing different states of grief, and for this reason I use them here.

Shock and denial

Shock is almost inevitable if the death had come suddenly or unexpectedly. Shock can be regarded as a physiological trauma that seems almost to overload the system. The news is too much to take in. There are two possible outward reactions: an unnerving feeling of composure and normality, or near hysteria.

At this stage you have little or no control over the way you behave. I remember being almost unable to move or speak when the doctors came in from the Intensive Care Unit to tell us the news, even though I had known that the end was near. It was only later when I had completed the formalities and was in the hospital car park that I broke down totally, in a near panic of confusion and anxiety.

Because of the enormity of what has happened it is more than likely that at first you will be unable to accept the reality of death. In fact, you may find yourself refusing to accept your situation. However, it is essential, if you are to start recovering from the shock you've had, that you take in the truth and admit that you will not be able to change what has happened. This is not easy to do, but if you do not acknowledge that this is the case, and resist it, then it is almost certain that the stresses and anxieties that will inevitably build up within you will lead to a severe strain on your bodily and psychological resources.

Denial is all too easy. We are surrounded by an elaborate codified language of death that is used to cloud reality and to create a distance between ourselves and it. We talk of the 'chapel of rest', 'to rest in peace', 'to sleep peacefully', 'to be at rest', 'eternal rest' or 'not dead but sleeping'. However, exhaustion and emotional collapse are certain outcomes of a prolonged period of refusal to accept the inevitable. More common reactions are a desire to withdraw socially, feeling unable to cope with the new responsibilities that you've inherited after a loved one's death, or being incapable of making even simple decisions. You have *no choice* but to accept and adapt to your new, unwanted circumstances. And the sooner you do so, the better.

Anger

Very soon after you have partially recovered from the shock of death, you may experience an anger that spills over into an almost uncontrollable rage. The anger may be directed against yourself – for example, if you were not with your son when he died and feel you could have prevented what happened by some action or other, or that you should have had enough money to hire the services of a famous specialist who might have been able to save or prolong your partner's life. Perversely, you may direct your anger against the loved one who has died: Why did he leave me to face the world all alone? Why did she deprive me of the chance to see her grow up/to fulfil all the plans we'd made together, etc? How could he be so *selfish*?

The explanation for this ill will is hurt, and the cause of your hurt is, in an indirect fashion, the person who has died. Anger may be the result of a sad misunderstanding in the last few hours or minutes of your loved one's life. A last kiss or squeeze of the hand may not have been acknowledged by the dying person. And since the bereaved are so sensitive to any clues about how they are valued by their loved one, so close to death, this can feel like a massive rejection. In reality, it may be that they had no energy to respond, or they needed to save their strength to deal with their oncoming death. But such rational understanding is virtually impossible at times like this.

Don't be surprised if you find yourself dwelling on the more negative aspects of their character, or re-running specific incidents in your head from your life together when, for example, you thought they didn't behave as they should have, or when they dismissed as trivial something you strongly believed in. Perhaps you nursed them for years at home and feel angry for having had this time 'taken away' from you. This seeming disavowal of your love is a common emotional self-defence strategy among the recently bereaved.

There are more obvious targets for anger. If death was tragically caused by a third party in a car crash or murder, for example, then your anger will be directed there. Violent fantasies of revenge against those who caused the death of your loved one can be extreme and all-enveloping.

It may be hospital staff, including the doctors and nurses, who are the prime objects of your anger, especially if you believe that, for whatever reason, they were able to prevent, or were negligent in causing, the death of your loved one. If you believe in a god, then you may direct your anger there. If your loved one died young, you might even look at elderly people in the street and ask yourself: 'Why didn't *they* die instead? They've already *had* their time.'

Much anger of this type is based on prejudice and misperceptions of reality. In the vast majority of cases, the causes of your anger are likely to be spurious and, ultimately, self-defeating. No amount of rage will make any difference to the reality that death has separated you from the person you loved. The only result of prolonged and irrational rage is bitterness, hatred, resentment (on your part *and* on the part of those who have had to listen to your rage) and probable ill health. The first step is to recognize that you are angry. It is only then that you will be able to release your anger in a constructive fashion.

Nevertheless, there may be times when you feel you just can't help yourself. It is quite likely that you will feel furious hostility welling up within you when you see people you know in the weeks following the funeral – at the supermarket, in the street, at work and at parties.

These are awkward moments, but it is important to keep in mind that it is possibly as difficult (if not *more* so) for them as it is for you. You will have had a little time to begin to adjust to your present state while they will have been becoming increasingly anxious about seeing you again. They will have been dreading it for fear of saying the wrong thing and upsetting you. And when they *do* eventually meet you they may feel that they are unable to cope. Some people *cannot* cope. I particularly remember, for instance, bumping into an acquaintance in the street fairly soon after Shirin's death. I saw the panic in her eyes before she looked away and strode off as fast as she could without saying anything.

These uncomfortable and embarrassing encounters continue as you begin to return to work and start going to social gatherings. Your colleagues at work might avoid you. You might see people at parties visibly stiffen as you walk into a room, as they steel themselves for what they anticipate will be an awkward interchange.

Almost inevitably, people are nervous and try to say something comforting, but mostly it just turns out to be foolish. For example, people commonly ask: 'Are you all right?' (I could hardly believe that so many people thought that this was an appropriate thing to ask because even in the fog of the earliest days of my despair it was obvious to me that this was a breathtakingly stupid question. My wife had just died. *Of course* I wasn't 'all right'.) Yet there is worse. 'Have you got over it yet?', 'I suppose that it's just one of those things', and 'Never mind' are examples.

There will be others you talk to who will try to rationalize the senselessness of death. For instance, I was told by a colleague that there *was* a purpose to Shirin's life and death. It was to make me 'grow as a person'. And while I'm able to understand an argument that suffering *might* lead to a greater understanding of self, I certainly didn't appreciate such trite, unsolicited and altogether dubious homespun philosophy. What such people do not realize is that someone in extreme grief doesn't want to know what they might have *gained* as a result of a tragedy; the bereaved are only concerned about what they have *lost*.

Even after a year or more, people presume to intrude on your grief. I remember being frustrated by something or other at work well into the second year after my wife's death, only to be told in the comforting tones reserved for the very smallest of children: 'Get over it, Hamish. After all, it was a *long* time ago.'

Feeling hurt by these sorts of 'well-intentioned' comments is not unusual. In fact you should expect it. However, if you find that your reaction to hurtful comments is to become antagonistic, you might want to consider reframing your thoughts. Instead of choosing to become incensed, a more constructive approach would be to empathize with the predicament of your workmates and acquaintances. Try and appreciate the apprehension that they are experiencing; they are only trying to do the best that they can. No-one, except an intensely callous person, would intentionally offend someone who has recently been bereaved. Don't strike out or think bitter thoughts; accept the attempts, however clumsy, of one individual trying to offer comfort and support to another.

Relief and guilt

Death is often sudden, but sadly, some people have to endure a great deal of suffering before they die. For some terminally ill patients, doctors may only be able to relieve pain and distress. Others, such as victims of multiple sclerosis or of the AIDS virus, suffer the progressive degeneration of their bodies. Others still, might recognize the onset of senile dementia. They may feel that they are, or will be, a burden to friends and family.

When the terminally ill partner, friend or family member dies you may experience a great sense of relief that can manifest itself in two forms. The first is on an immediate level of thankfulness that he or she is no longer suffering, feels no pain and is at peace. The second level seems more insidious because you may find yourself thinking that your suffering has ended too. You no longer have to devote your life to caring for, feeding, washing or dressing the loved one, who may not even have recognised you towards the end. All the days, months or years of watching their physical or mental deterioration are over. It is no surprise that you feel relief. Associated with the relief you feel at the release of your loved one's pain, however, will be guilt. This brings pain, but it's important to realize that only a saint would feel *no* resentment at having to look after a sick partner or forgive and forget *all* their imperfections. Every human relationship is bound together with conflicting feelings of love and occasional dislike. And after someone you love dies it's normal to feel guilt at having had some feelings of dislike for them when they were alive. Recognize this, and forgive yourself for experiencing almost inevitable negative reactions when death occurs.

Sadness and despair

For a long time after the death of someone close to you, you will feel extremely sad. This sadness is more commonly known as depression, which is a clinical neurosis and not just 'feeling a bit down'. Depression is not a mental disorder but a condition caused by circumstances and the depressed person's inability to adapt to them. Most people who suffer depression as a reaction to the death of a loved one experience it in a mild form – although, of course, there will be some people who have a more extreme response. The usual signs of depression are fatigue, social withdrawal, disinterest in your surroundings, not caring about how you look or your general health, insomnia and a tendency to brood.

The danger with depression is that in cases where the bereaved lives alone or is otherwise isolated, the cycle of neglect is unbroken, which may lead to increased depression, possible abuse of drugs and/or alcohol, and/or an exhibition of extreme and unbalanced behaviour. The ultimate expression of depression is despair and suicide. Evidence suggests that elderly widows have a higher suicide rate than those who have not been widowed. Similarly, elderly widowers, who may have lost their sole emotional confidante as well as closest companion, seem likely to experience a loneliness that drives them towards suicidal thoughts. Still, the overwhelming majority of people who are recovering from the shock of a bereavement do not attempt suicide. But do not be surprised if you entertain morbid thoughts of taking your own life. Such gruesome fantasies are common.

It is relatively simple to counter the mild depression associated with bereavement. The answer is to keep busy and try to do something that increases your self-esteem, since the death of someone close to you inevitably lowers your feelings of self-worth. However, if the intensity of your depression is such that getting involved in your work, hobbies, pastimes or looking after your health doesn't seem to help, consult your doctor. More extreme depression requires medical attention from experts, which is normally very effective. The treatment should not be seen as evidence of mental incapacity on your part. A depression that is the result of the death of a loved one is a natural occurrence and will be well understood by any good doctor.

Anxiety

Anxieties associated with bereavement range from the major to the trivial. When one partner dies, for example, it often happens that the surviving partner feels they are unable to cope with all of the obligations and demands of the future, especially when they do not have the support of their partner to help and guide them. This fear of the future can be so terrifying that the person lies awake at night so tense with worry that they almost feel on the verge of emotional collapse. Their anxieties might include worrying about being able to pay a mortgage, distress at being forced into unwanted work in order to make ends meet, or even fear over how to change fuses in a fuse box if they've never done it before.

If you've lost a child you could feel anxious that you might not be able to look after surviving children properly, or even those you might intend to have in the future. A young child might have deep and often unrealistic worries concerning death itself, and might feel that either they have somehow contributed to a person's death or that they or people close to them will die soon. A friend or sibling might worry that others will be judging their emotional reactions after a death as being too distant or insincere.

Quite simply, someone who has been bereaved may feel that they may be losing their mind, or believe that they are just unable to cope with the future. Their great anxiety is that of breaking down and being incapable of functioning from one day to the next. Of course, in the majority of cases, the reality is the opposite. However, the fact that the person is experiencing fears out of proportion to the reality of the situation is the defining characteristic of anxiety.

Initially, the scale of worry that you might feel you have to face will be enormous. It might make you feel indecisive, helpless and useless, which in turn feeds your anxiety. But over the weeks and the months that follow you will *have to* confront these fears and, in confronting them, you will find that they will diminish. Perhaps the greatest aid in combating anxiety is being able to relax. Relaxation is a series of skills that can be learnt and practised at almost any time of the day. When you are able to relax you will be able to tackle you fears head on and, in tackling them, you will find that they disappear. See Chapter 5 on relaxation and meditation techniques for more ideas.

Acceptance and strength

Be assured that you will *never* be the same after the death of your loved one. The death of someone close to you is not something that anyone 'gets over'. In fact, it's something that most people don't *want* to get over. Getting over something implies forgetting about it and the last thing that you'll want to do is to forget about your wife, husband, father, mother, brother, sister or friend. This in turn does not mean that someone who has recently been bereaved should live by, or in, the past. The aim is to accept that they have gone, draw strength from the past and let go of the pain.

The ideal, perhaps, is to have joyful, invigorating memories of the past with no diminishing of the present. Strength comes from memories of shared experiences. These *can* be the memories of single, frivolous incidents that made both of you laugh, but perhaps more important are the memories of significant incidents that reinforced the beliefs in the values that you shared in your relationship. Typically, these might include: honesty, integrity, supportiveness, respect, trust and devotion.

These memories will help in two ways. When you feel yourself slipping into pessimism and depression they will remind you of how you loved, and *were* loved, and will sustain you in what will be exceptionally difficult times.

two

Patterns of death and grief

It is not possible to describe every kind of loss or every way in which people grieve. Death comes in all forms, and people react in countless ways. For each individual, the death and loss of a loved one is unique, and grieved for in a wholly distinctive fashion. However, it *is* possible to focus on similarities in broad categories of grief, and show ways that could help in resolving them.

The following sections provide a framework to patterns of death and grief that can be applied to the commonality of many other people's experiences.

Losing a child

It is significant that the death of a child is not just the tragedy of stillbirth, cot death, or illnesses or accidents that take the life of a young girl or boy, or adolescent. A child is a child at thirty or forty to the parents of that adult. And when adults die there is often a parent, or parents, left to grieve.

The death of a child is especially brutal because it's untimely, in that it upsets the concept of a 'natural' order of life and death wherein parents die before their children. For this reason alone, perhaps, there is no greater grief than the grief following the death of a child. It's a crushing upset from which many people feel they do not fully recover. This is especially true if the death is accompanied, as it often is, by intense feelings of guilt, regret and failure.

Death of a foetus or newborn baby

While the loss of a child throws up unique issues whatever the child's age, there do appear to be special problems associated with the death of a child during pregnancy, or soon after birth. If your child died a very early death it's likely that your feelings of being somehow at fault are intense. This may be because parents *are* parents, and the duty of parents is to be able to provide for their children. In a sense parents are the ones whose duty it is to 'fix' it so that their child will have a safe environment in which to grow up. Sadly, parents simply *cannot* fix everything. Miscarriage, stillbirth, neonatal death and cot death (otherwise known as Sudden Infant Death Syndrome or SIDS) are often wholly unpredictable. They are therefore unpreventable.

Nevertheless, the shock of saying goodbye to a dear child before having said hello is devastating. This sense of loss and aloneness may be amplified by the staggeringly insensitive and unhelpful comments of others. Choice among these are: 'Don't worry. You can have another one', or 'I know it's sad, but it's not as if you really *knew* the baby'. The expectation of those who have not suffered such a loss seems to be that the bonds of parenthood are somehow more valid if the child who died was at least a toddler, or boy or girl of primary school age. The reality is different. Attachment to a child usually begins even before it is born – a mother is likely to recognize her foetus as an individual.

The background to the death, when it occurs in the hospital, may be cloudy. Mothers are often sedated. They may not be given the option of holding their dead child, as some hospitals continue the practice of routinely cremating foetuses and the stillborn, even though many foetuses are well formed by twenty-eight weeks. Mothers may feel particularly bereft if they have no token to indicate that their baby existed at all. It is natural and comforting to cherish a lock of hair, a photograph or an inky foot- or hand-print on a piece of paper. They may have nothing except the memory of a small white coffin, and a short, sad service just before the burial or cremation of their child.

All of this can cause specific patterns of grief in parents whose children die very young. In addition to thoughts of anger, guilt and depression there is often a profound sense of 'what might have been'. Linked to this are private fantasies of what the child could have achieved. This can add to feelings of being detached socially, and from reality, which in turn fuel fears of going slightly crazy.

It's not too surprising, therefore, to find that couples find it difficult to talk to each other about the death of their baby. But there is a further problem in that fathers are unlikely to have formed as strong an attachment to the baby as the mother at the earliest stages. As a result, marriages after a stillbirth or SIDS death can suffer severe trauma.

Clearly, recovery after the early death of a child is by no means easy, but there are positive steps you can take which will help to rebuild your life:

- **Hold the baby** If possible, and the doctors agree, hold your baby. For a few minutes look upon your child as having been born; cradle the baby gently in your arms, and caress him or her. This might seem a strange thing to suggest, but it is important for mothers to form a final attachment with their baby, and for fathers to be given an opportunity to develop an emotional bond with their child. This provides a sensitive and very human closing to life that will serve as a small, yet significant, memory that will sustain you in grief. Take photographs, ask for a lock of hair, or a print of your baby's hand or foot.

- **Help plan the funeral** The funeral provides an opportunity to say goodbye to your baby. Normally, hospitals will provide such a service free for foetal deaths and neonatal deaths. They use the services of a contract undertaker for a specific cemetery. Remember that you are not obliged to accept these arrangements if you believe they are unsatisfactory for any reason. It may be that you disapprove of the cemetery itself or the style of service it offers. If the thought of a white coffin is too harsh a container for a child that has not tasted much of life, you could consider using something that has altogether less jarring imagery and connotations. This could simply be a soft shawl or shroud, or other cloth. Ask if you can personally place the body in the grave; you can ensure that it is a 'natural' position. Choosing a private ceremony might also mean fewer restrictions on the placing of tokens of love, such as teddies and dollies, by the grave. In making a private arrangement you could think about buying an adult grave so that you can be buried with your child when you die.

- **Remember** Naturally, you will want to remember your baby. However, the best way to remember your baby is *not* to succumb to the temptation to make a shrine out of a nursery that you might have prepared in anticipation of your baby's birth. There will come a time when you will have to reappraise the value of keeping hold of what could have been, and remember your baby in more healthy and positive ways. These may include simply looking at what photographs or other remembrances you may have, and openly (without bitter regret) talking with your partner of what hopes you had for your child. But more than this, you could add to the memory of your child by giving gifts to organizations that help needy children throughout the world. You could choose significant dates such as Christmas or the birthday of your child to do this.

Guilt feelings

It is important for someone who has lost a child to deal with feelings of guilt for not having done something to prevent it. Feelings of having failed or having done something wrong can be deep-set. Perhaps the best way of overcoming these thoughts is to find out as much as you can about the death. If your child died in hospital, ask the doctors to explain as clearly as possible what happened. You might have to rephrase your questions several times; some doctors are good at communicating, others are not. Ask them if there was anything that could realistically have been done to make a difference.

A 'difference' does not mean your child's life would necessarily have been saved by another form of, or quicker, intervention. For example, when my wife died we asked a lot of questions in the weeks and months afterwards. We found out that even if Shirin *had* been given a liver transplant, which the doctors were in the process of setting up when she died, it's likely that this would only have prolonged her life rather than saved it. She would also only have been sustained by a variety of drugs, primarily steroids, which would themselves have produced severe adverse reactions.

There were other questions that we asked which the doctors had no answer to. Sometimes there are *no* answers. Sadly, there are not always obvious reasons for a person's death. It's no-one's fault; no-one's to blame. Even so, as parents, the future is undermined. A spark of joy is extinguished; never again will you share the beauty of your child's life.

The grief of siblings

In the despair following a child's death, the grief of the surviving children can easily be overlooked, since friends and relatives generally pay their respects to the parents first, and only afterwards to the children. If the surviving child or children are teenagers or younger, they may hardly be acknowledged at all except with a passing 'Are the children coping?'

Perhaps, if it was pointed out to someone that this attitude was slightly thoughtless, they might dispute it, saying that the parent–child relationship is the most significant – a sibling is someone who's 'just' lost a brother or sister. The received wisdom appears to be that the grief of a parent who has lost a child is greater than the grief of a sibling of that child.

But a sibling's grief is not 'greater' or 'lesser' than a parent's; it's simply different. And, regardless of whether they got on with their brother or sister when they were alive, it's very real. They have lost someone who shared a common bond and background. Despite this, many surviving children feel they can't express their feelings to the rest of the family, which in turn increases their sense of frustration, anger and resentment at being left alone to deal with their grief.

In many cases they are expected to help their parents grieve, and this can be a heavy burden because they feel that they always have to be upbeat for their parents' sake while keeping their own grief private. Don't forget that children can experience acute feelings of guilt as well, especially if they fostered long-term ill will against their brother or sister. For other siblings, who have lost a close companion who shared a special bond during childhood and adult life, there can be intense and long-term feelings of regret. These feelings often emerge at significant points in the surviving sibling's life when it's apparent that their brother or sister is not there to share in the joy, say, of a marriage, birth of a child, or even moving to a new place and starting an exciting new job.

Surviving siblings also tend to believe that the favourite or 'wrong' child died. So, if your other (particularly younger) children begin to adopt the personality and habits of their dead brother or sister, it may be an attempt to lessen your pain as parents. To the same end, other surviving children temporarily assume parental roles when adults cannot cope. This may happen particularly at significant family occasions such as birthdays and family reunions.

So, remember to include your children, and talk with them when they need it, but remember that they also need space. Allow *them* to grieve.

Terminal illness

Terminally ill adults

Perhaps the most important factor in relation to terminal illness is for you and your loved one to maintain a belief and dignity in life until death comes, despite possible increasing pain, and decreasing autonomy. For some people for whose illness there is no cure, the needs of security and support are not necessarily provided by a conventional hospital. Hospital staff don't have the luxury of time to devote to dying patients or their loved ones. The primary aim of a hospital is medical and physical intervention, without necessarily taking into account the emotional needs of the patient or those closest to them.

An alternative is hospice care. The approach of a hospice is to alleviate suffering through medical intervention, and to maintain the dignity of the person who is dying while giving support to their family. A collaborative programme of care is developed, and the family is consulted and included in providing support for their loved one. The intention is to allow the patient to die with dignity, and in an atmosphere of humanity.

However, regardless of whether your loved one is in a hospital, a hospice, or at home, they will probably exhibit the fears and needs common to those in their position. It's possible to identify these, and, with the assistance of professional carers, offer them some help in coping with a whole range of issues. Apart from the illness itself, these can include the sometimes painful diagnostic procedures, treatments such as radiation or chemotherapy, and turbulent emotional states including a sense of worthlessness, aloneness and a need to tidy up the loose ends of life.

- **Fear of being alone** One of the greatest fears of people who have been told, or believe, that they are dying is that they may die alone. Sometimes they feel that any physical deterioration may turn people away; they fear that they might become too repulsive, or ugly, or too much of a burden. In a sense this is true. Often, when death is inevitable or draws near, friends and relatives outside the immediate family tend to disengage themselves, and draw away from the dying person on the assumption that they would want to be alone in order to prepare themselves for death. There may be additional factors that influence whether or not people visit the dying person. For example, the continuing stigma of a disease such as AIDS might keep potential visitors away from a dying AIDS patient. But a person who is dying needs the love and support of their closest and dearest. It's a very human need. They need you to be there to appreciate them, to reminisce, to cry and to laugh.

- **Feelings of worthlessness**   Up until the time they started to become ill, people who are dying had a more positive self-image, and a greater sense of worth as members of their family and society. However, their illness may have led to a gradual physical deterioration to the point that they are unable to go to work or even live at home. Whereas previously they may have had important jobs, or contributed to the household as a decision-maker or bread-winner, these roles are gone. With these, all too easily, goes their positive self-image. It won't help their feelings of uselessness to say: 'Don't waste your time thinking about these little things. You just concentrate on conserving your energy. Don't waste it.' You can help restore their spirits and feelings of self-worth by finding ways to fully involve them in making many of the important everyday decisions that involve family members and finances. You could draw up a list of decisions that need to be made, or an account of expenses that need to be sorted out, and find a regular time to discuss them. Naturally, they should be fully consulted in all the medical decisions made on their behalf.

- **A need to 'tidy up'**   For those adults who recognize that they are dying, there is usually a need to put their affairs in order. This can take the form of writing a will, planning the funeral or making sure that the family is financially secure or

24

employed. It can also involve a desire to release old resent-ments, and to resolve any outstanding personal or family feuds that may exist. These issues can be painful, not only because of what might be said, but also because this might seem as though they are somehow 'giving in' to death or abandoning hope. This probably isn't the case; when people feel they are near death they can feel an extreme need to tie up the loose ends of their life. Their attitude may be rather businesslike, but that's only because they know that there's so little time left. You'll help in being similarly pragmatic in order to bring them towards a sense of closure and inner peace. (For further dis-cussion of wills and funerals, see Chapter 3.)

Terminally ill children

Younger children tend to have a very clear notion of causation, and commonly believe that since no-one else is to blame for their illness, they somehow are responsible for bad things happening to them. They may not openly say this, but it's likely that these thoughts will be deeply troubling them. Questions like: 'Why am I ill?' or 'What's happening to me?' can be coded messages from children, inviting reassurance rather than a straightforward expla-nation of what's happening to their bodies. One way of gently opening up these thoughts, and resolving these fears, is to turn questions like these on their head and ask your child why *they* think they're ill or what could be happening to them. Thus they have the opportunity to express what is *really* worrying them.

This doesn't mean, of course, that children don't worry about what's happening to their bodies. They do. In cases where there are multiple treatments, constant side-effects, and occasional relapses and failures, it can feel to the child that their body no longer belongs to them, but somehow is the property of the doc-tors and nurses. Very young children can become extremely upset when medical staff have to take blood samples, not understanding that their bodies can replace any blood that's taken from them.

Furthermore, children also may be aware that they will die. They will be anxious about this even though they might not openly say so.

All of these constitute delicate subjects that should be treated according to your child's age and understanding, and in a spirit of honesty, reassurance and supportiveness. Children aren't incapable of understanding what's happening, and, like an adult, can feel very alone and fearful. They need to be listened to, by you and by professionals, and be given guidance on how to face their illness, and to live optimistically despite it.

Friends and family

Of course, not all of the difficulties of terminal illness relate solely to the patient. Friends and family are also affected. If you have been aware of the nature of your loved one's illness, you will have been anticipating their death. It's only natural, but it makes an already distressing ordeal all the more demanding. This is because in anticipating the death it's likely that you will have been feeling guilty at thinking about the practical issues of how you will live your life after they are dead even while they are still alive. It seems as though you're being disloyal in letting go before you're supposed to.

But, again, this is to be expected. There is an inevitable conflict between looking after someone who is dying, and the need to reorder your life. It's a pre-death reshuffling of roles that happens when people recognize that someone they love is dying that is similar to post-death grief. However, the two processes shouldn't be confused, in the sense that in anticipating what happens after the death you will somehow subsequently grieve less. There isn't a fixed amount of grieving that takes place when someone dies. You'll just grieve differently, that's all.

Facing grief after a suicide

Coping with a death that was self-inflicted is extremely difficult. It seems to be beyond question that the stresses on a family where a death is a result of suicide are greater than those imposed by most other forms of death. A great deal depends on the age of the person who takes their life, but in all cases the reactions of family members and friends are likely to be harsh and complex.

Stresses

In addition to dealing with the range of emotions that all the bereaved have to cope with, the families of a suicide face other extreme stresses. Typically they include:

- **Denial** In common with those who have become bereaved under less tragic circumstances, the families of suicides find it difficult to accept that their loved one has died. Yet, more than this, it's not unusual for them to deny that the death was due to suicide at all. If the suicide was a teenager or young adult, his or her father tends to take it very badly. Of all of the family members it's fathers who typically deny the fact of suicide the most. Even when they become more accepting, they commonly rationalize the act of suicide. Instead of recognizing in the tragedy any internal family problem or other unreleased pressures, outside factors such as drugs in society, the company that the suicide kept, and the breakdown of society as a whole are blamed.

- **Shame**   There is such stigma attached to suicide that one of the most powerful emotional reactions to an act of suicide within the family is shame. Registrars are routinely asked to falsify death certificates by grieving family members who don't want the truth to emerge publicly. Even within the family there is often a conspiracy of silence to keep the dread secret. To

27

neighbours and acquaintances, the death is passed off as an 'accident'.

- **Guilt**   The guilt in the aftermath of a suicide is unlike the regrets and guilt associated with other forms of death. Instead of bitter regrets over a catalogue of actions or arguments, you might feel almost overpowering guilt not only for what you feel you should have done to prevent the suicide, but also for what you might have done that *contributed* to its happening. The guilt of parents whose children have taken their own lives may be extreme. Western society holds that they are responsible for the upbringing of children, and with the suicide they are deemed to have failed as stable, nurturing parents. Similarly, adult children may feel overwhelming guilt if their elderly, recently widowed parent died by suicide. They will inevitably feel they should have visited them more often. Partners of suicides may feel a peculiarly acute form of guilt since they more than anyone should have 'seen the signs'.

- **Fear**   A darker, and perhaps more disturbing, reaction to suicide is the fear that it can unleash. Primarily, this is the fear of self and of an individual's impulse to self-destruct, but in addition it is the fear that someone else in the family might take their own life.

  Perhaps more tragic, and very real, is the constant fear that people outside the family will discover the fact of the suicide and almost inevitably interpret it in such a way as to negatively affect the family's social standing. There seems little doubt that someone who dies as a result of an accident, illness, old age or even violence is more likely to be viewed with sympathy than someone who takes their own life. The act is often interpreted by others as a shocking and violent end to a tragic story of rejection or abuse by (usually) the suicide's father, and is symptomatic of a dysfunctional family.

  These perceptions are increased if the suicide act of your loved one required some determination and energy, such as hanging, as opposed to a more passive end through taking an overdose of pills. Furthermore, even if there are mitigating factors, such as the proven psychological instability of the suicide, these tend not to alter an outsider's interpretation of events.

Strategies for coping

Given these stresses, it is immensely difficult for those left behind to pick up the pieces of their lives, and start to recover. It's quite possible that specialist help will be necessary to overcome the barriers of silence inside the family, and feelings of public isolation. However, regardless of whether a specialist is brought in, there are a number of strategies that you can use to help cope with your loss:

- **Talk** Make sure that the family talks about what has happened. It's important for everyone to show each other constructive support at this time. This is especially true in the first few days following the death since this is a time when feelings of guilt, and bitter accusations of blame, are likely to surface and stifle and ensnare a family in a cycle of unhealthy recrimination.

- **Be objective** It is common for survivors of an adult suicide to view the death, and the person, in extreme terms. This can result in seeing your loved one as having had an almost saint-like personality. In addition, survivors often assume *total* responsibility for not having foreseen the act itself, and blame themselves for not having 'done enough' to prevent it. While sadly there is sometimes good reason for such guilt, it is important to realize that suicide is not necessarily motivated by a feeling of not being supported by others, but can be a result of an unseen accumulation of stresses, or by psychiatric disorders and personality factors that probably could not have been influenced by immediate family members. It is essential to correct distorted guilt patterns and reassess attitudes so that the fact of suicide, and objective feelings of guilt, can be accepted as soon as possible. With acceptance and understanding, it is more likely that a sense of peace will follow.

- **Allow yourself to be angry**   In tandem with a sense of wanting to idealize your loved one, it is likely that you will find yourself becoming intensely angry with them. You may be furious at your son for not having tried to communicate his problems and needs before he took his life. If your partner was a suicide, you may feel rage within you that she left you (or your relatives) with children to bring up, a mess of legal and financial issues to deal with. You may simply feel rage at the seeming waste of life itself. It is perfectly normal for suicide survivors to experience an almost terrifying anger. Permit yourself this emotion.

Euthanasia

It must be pointed out, however, that not all forms of suicide are necessarily incomprehensible or hugely traumatic. The arguments in favour of active euthanasia, or 'assisted suicide' as it seems to be becoming more widely known, are fairly straightforward. Under circumstances of advanced terminal illness that causes intolerable pain and suffering to an individual, or when physical handicap is deemed too restrictive by an individual, despite lengthy consideration, counselling, physiotherapy and other intervention, then it is the right of a mature, rational adult in the face of hopelessness to take their own life. Supporters do not believe euthanasia should be used as a first resort when the knowledge of certain death from illness becomes apparent.

Perhaps because of the voluntary and rational nature of euthanasia the emotions of shame, guilt and fear may be lessened for those left behind, knowing that their loved one's life ended under their own control, and without undue suffering. This would be especially true if your loved one made a Living Will indicating that they accepted the notion of taking their own life in a calm and orderly fashion. A Living Will is a document that outlines the circumstances in which the person who draws it up wishes medical intervention to be limited or stopped altogether.

Opponents of euthanasia see this form of suicide as being unjustifiable from a number of different perspectives. Perhaps chief among these is that the practice of pain management and relief available in hospices is excellent. There are also those who reject euthanasia on ethical and theological grounds. They would suggest that it is the duty of doctors not to take life, but to preserve it, and to leave the matters of life and death to a god.

Grieving and children

All too often children are cosseted instead of being brought into the grieving process. The justification for this decision is outwardly entirely rational: 'Don't upset the child.' But, of course, the death of a family member or friend has short- and long-term effects for a child just as it has for an adult. There may be emotional difficulties for them at school and later, as young adults, it's possible that they will suffer a loss of self-esteem and a profound sense of aloneness.

Losing a parent

Instead of being shut out by the surviving parent, it is important for the child to be included in the grieving process from the start. High on the list of priorities for the surviving parent is the need to assure the child that he or she will be looked after, cared for and loved. This in itself might be problematic since a surviving parent may feel ill-equipped, as far as having all the skills necessary to care for and support the child or children, and, at the same time, to hold down a job. However, don't be afraid to take your children into your confidence. Make time each day to sit with your children and talk over what has happened.

On a more practical level, even if the children are small, you might have to ask them to take on some more household responsibilities. This will not only give you all the chance to understand that you are still working together as part of a family, but also give you a framework to talk about the significant, though less serious, events that are part of everyday life. But remember that if you *do* ask your children to shoulder more of the day-to-day chores, it's best if you are consistent in the demands you make of them. In other words, don't impose extra work on them just because you may be busy at the time.

The child will have a lot of questions about the death that will probably be disturbingly frank: When? Where? How? and Why? These should be answered as openly and as honestly as possible. Perhaps most important of all, the distinction between the temporary and permanent absence of the parent should be made evident. This can be difficult with the very young. Children under the age of five have a poor understanding of the permanence of death and are likely to think of it as extended sleep. As a result they may even worry about sleeping themselves. Often the very young believe that death is a planned act for which someone is responsible. They may even feel that *they* are responsible in some way.

Those who are a little older realize that death is final. However, they may seem morbidly interested in the process of the body's decay rather than simply wanting to grieve. This may be because they tend to view death in very impersonal terms; it's something that happens to other (and older) people. For this reason they find it interesting, but in what can seem to be a cold and heartless way. It's possible that their impressions of death may be distorted by what they experience through television or the snippets of adults' discussions about death they overhear.

Children of about 9–11 begin to realize that death is not only permanent, but also irreversible. They also have an understanding that it's something that could happen to them. However, it's not their death that worries them so much as the possibility that one or both of *their* parents will die – and soon. Some children attempt to hide their fears by joking about death or pretending to be perfectly indifferent to it.

Like adults, children experience similar stages of the grieving process, but can react differently. This is because they have limited experience of life and find it difficult to express the confused jumble of emotions they feel. Extremes of behaviour are common. They may at turns seem very upset and then totally disinterested in what has happened. They may want to talk about the person who's died all the time or conversely not at all. There may be similar reactions in their attitudes to schoolwork. Almost inevitably there will be some children who constantly want attention or complain of minor illnesses such as headaches or stomach upsets.

Sometimes these extreme reactions can persist and deepen. Some children may exhibit a constant and unreasonable anger towards everyone and everything. This may be manifested in shouting or screaming or in physical attacks on siblings or friends. Sadly, animals are often the victim of a child's confused state; they can feel that it's acceptable to take out their anger on a family's pet or to shoot at birds with a catapult or air gun. Depression for children can be a real problem. They may isolate themselves from all their friends and family, develop an extreme fear of going to school, and threaten suicide. If you feel your child's behaviour goes beyond a normal expression of grief then consider outside help.

Helpful concepts

Of course, there is a great deal that you can do to help your child yourself. Apart from answering questions as honestly and as fully as you can, you can help by explaining the following concepts:

- **Death is inevitable**   All living things must die. It's a natural process. People don't die because they've done, thought or said something wrong and are being punished for it.

- **Death is irreversible**   It's important to make sure that the child isn't suffering the delusion that if they wish the person back enough they will return. Sometimes children can be confused by the permanence of death and feel bewilderment, hurt or intense anger when, for example, their parent doesn't reappear as they used to after a business trip.

- **Death is for a reason**   Some children find it difficult to accept that illness, accidents or old age are straightforward reasons to die. It needs to be emphasized that the illness or accident didn't happen because that person wasn't 'good' enough to live. Similarly, though it may seem almost callous to even consider it, violent death through murder is a reason to die. It's important for children to realize this because they often feel that they caused the death because they thought 'bad' things.

- **Death means that all functions of life cease**   A child's world is a very sensory one, full of movement and activity. Some children, who do not understand that all the sensory functions of life and all thought processes end with death, become worried that the person may feel cold, hungry or have undergone great pain if the body was cremated, or not have enough air to breathe if it was buried.

Perhaps the most important thing is for you to be patient and be available to talk to the child and to share your own feelings of grief with them. This can encourage them to talk, understand and accept death. It's also a good idea to have a talk with the child's teachers at school. After all, teachers are significant adults in a child's life and can be a great help. They should be asked to make sure that while they should be flexible with the child as regards their school work, they should expect and encourage the child to *do* the work. Keeping busy is an essential strategy in preventing depression from taking too great a hold.

There are a number of other strategies that can encourage children to grieve in an inclusive, positive way. Together you can plant a tree or a bed of flowers in remembrance of the person who has died. Alternatively, you could help them create an album of photographs or paintings of your loved one; let the children have some input into the writing of any captions underneath the pictures. It can also help if you encourage the child to write down their feelings as a journal, poem or a story. Take some time not only with *what* is written, but also with the *way* it's presented. You could bind all of it into book form, with covers and, perhaps, a photograph of the person on the front.

Bereavement in old age

There can be severe emotional problems for older people after their partner dies. Some adjust very well to death, but in cases where partners have been together for many years, day-to-day living can be difficult. One reason, apart from loneliness, is that older couples are often mutually dependent, and the lack of support after a death can lead to chronic self-neglect. Why bother? time and life seem so pointless now. This reaction is common if one of a couple had to care for their partner for many months or years before they died. Tied to this is the burden of guilt at feelings of relief in seeing a partner's misery coming to an end. This is not to say that most who wish their partner dead are motivated by hate – quite the opposite – but it's characteristic of carers of the long-term ill to have such thoughts.

Practical problems

There are many practical problems for someone who has been bereaved in old age. Perhaps chief among these is loneliness, but there are other anxieties including concerns about health, possible financial difficulties, and issues of security. Here are a few suggestions to deal with these particular issues:

• **Loneliness**   The loneliness after bereavement in old age can be intense. It doesn't help that in Western society, where the extended family rarely lives together and may be quite widely scattered, widows and widowers almost invariably find themselves alone, and may become dangerously isolated. The sense of longing and loss is a feeling that some believe they can never get over. The only way to overcome loneliness is to work at it. Don't expect it to be easy. It won't be.

Early on it may also seem as though to have fun is somehow disloyal to the memory of your partner, but there may come a time when instead of becoming distraught, and wistfully reflecting: 'I wish she/he was here', you might begin to enjoy the activity itself without guilt and smile, and think: 'Yes, she/he would have liked this too.'

Lack of money or mobility also can make things difficult, but if you have some extra cash to spare you could think about going to evening classes at a local college or joining one of the extracurricular classes at a university. Some local councils subsidize such courses, and so they can be fairly cheap. The range of studies is huge; there's everything from learning how to upholster furniture to becoming computer literate or learning a new language. And, of course, it's a very good way of meeting people. If you're more mobile you could join a rambling club, a bowls club or a choir. Read the section 'Whole life support' (page 74) for more ideas.

- **Health**   Some researchers have concluded that elderly widows and widowers are more likely to suffer illness or die soon after a bereavement. A few put this down to a loss of will to live, or more simply put, a broken heart. Others suggest that any increase in visits to doctors in the six months after a bereavement can be put down to tension or anxiety, or symptoms of illness that were ignored just prior to their partner's death. Whatever the case, living by yourself is certainly difficult. Without a companion there doesn't seem much reason to get up, eat properly and get out and about. There are potential health risks in this. Simple things can help: eat properly balanced meals; make sure you exercise regularly; keep warm. See Chapter 8 *Looking after your health* for more ideas.

• **Money**   Money doesn't need to be tight for you to take advantage of any benefits that you might be entitled to. State grants or credit are not charity. If you are not very mobile or have medically-documented physical problems, you may be eligible for financial support. There is no shame in taking it. Similarly, if your partner served in any of the armed forces, you may be entitled to a sum of money as the widow of a war veteran.

• **Security**   It's a fact that most elderly people who have lost a partner are women. Women tend to live longer than men, and also to marry older men. By the age of seventy-five two-thirds of women have lost their husbands. Many women in this position, probably quite rightly, feel threatened and physically at risk. If you haven't already done so, install a chain on your door, and a fish-eye peephole, so that you can check on people who are calling. Put locks on all of the windows. Always ask to see the cards of any officials or workmen. If in doubt, call up their offices to be quite sure that they are legitimate. (Get the numbers from the telephone directory; any number you get from the person at the door might simply put you in touch with an accomplice.) Don't be put off by people complaining that you're being 'difficult'; you're just being safe. You could consider getting a dog. Get to know your neighbours, and let them know when you're going away so they can keep an eye on your place. A telephone is an essential tool in keeping in touch with officials and friends. Think seriously about getting a phone/fax machine, or a computer with a modem and e-mail (if you haven't got one already) as this makes communication easier.

Remember that your life still counts even though the death of your partner may have slightly shifted your perspective at present. You

37

still have the right to make choices and decisions, to be treated decently and with respect, and to have control over what happens to you. Being older can make it a little more difficult, perhaps because in Western society the elderly aren't valued as highly as they should be, but it is completely possible.

One way of starting to take control is to get organized. Arrange what you're going to do the next day each evening. This could be a part of a regular (possibly weekly) routine involving getting out for a walk every day with a purpose other than getting some fresh air, such as getting your pension, going to a class or an exhibition, or posting letters. Get some exercise, be curious and active. If you aren't so mobile, ask relatives and friends to help with things you can't do yourself. Alternatively, contact an association that represents elderly people for information and assistance (see the *Resources* section, page 158).

Unresolved grief

The majority of bereaved people eventually manage to get their lives together, and find that life is again meaningful. They realize that even though there will be no-one to replace their loved one, they will have new and fulfilling relationships with others and will develop new interests and hobbies. But some people are either unable or unwilling to end the grieving process. They find themselves locked into a cycle of excessive and chronic despair, guilt and anger.

As you might imagine, given the varied nature of people's circumstances, the process of grieving is not necessarily straightforward. Its normal progress can be disrupted by a variety of factors including the unspeakable nature of the death, the attitude of the people around the bereaved person, and a tendency, when people lose their partner, to distort the dead partner's qualities.

In rare cases, the suddenness, and sometimes violence, of death can create a crisis of such enormity that it can take a great deal of time for grief to be resolved. Murder, being burned to death, dying in a car or plane crash, or as an innocent bystander or victim of terrorist attack are examples. The facts, and the magnitude, of what has happened may go so far beyond the experiences of those who are left that they cannot cope. Fear, incomprehension, vulnerability, and an intense anger at anyone (or a god) who may be responsible, are probable emotional outcomes. In addition, if your loved one was murdered, or killed themselves, the stigma can be so strong that it can lead to even more protracted grief. The questions commonly asked by neighbours or acquaintances, for example: 'Why didn't you *do* something?' or 'Didn't you *know* they were going to kill themselves?', can stir intense feelings of guilt and shame.

It doesn't always end with only coming to terms with the death itself. The aftermath of such horrors in courtrooms, with officials, the police and the media can be as stressful and traumatic as the appalling events themselves. In these circumstances, it is likely that you would benefit from help by professionals who will provide an environment and support system for you to begin a full, healthy resolution to your grief. Refer to the *Resources* section at the back of this book for addresses of useful organizations.

Unsatisfactory support

However, in more normal circumstances, one of the main reasons for an abnormally lengthy period of grieving is the lack of the right kind of support from friends and family. Some relatives and friends, with the best of intentions, don't allow the bereaved person to talk about the death of their loved one. They fall silent when this 'difficult' subject is broached because they don't want to risk 'upsetting' the bereaved. They forget that it is probably next to impossible to get more upset than the bereaved already is.

Other sets of family and friends go to the other extreme. They lavish excessive attention on the bereaved for an extended period that sometimes prevents them from starting work again or from renewing their old interests and friendships. They might insist: 'Not yet. You're not ready yet.'

This over-concern, while again undertaken with the interests of the bereaved at heart, unfortunately prevents the healthy and steady maturation of the grieving process. It goes against the advice of psychologists, who suggest that the most productive and supportive climate for the bereaved is one where they are able to acknowledge and express their feelings. During this process tears will fall, but this isn't a case of getting more upset, it's just a part of the process of recovery. And instead of smothering the bereaved with attention, it would be more appropriate for the bereaved to be encouraged to find practical solutions to the difficulties they face in returning to 'ordinary' everyday life.

Bereaved partners

There are also issues that arise in the recovery period that relate specifically to bereaved partners. It sometimes happens that over time the image they have of their deceased partner becomes so distorted that it interferes with the successful formation of new relationships. In effect, the deceased partner is 'sanctified' by the surviving partner. They habitually compare any new person they meet with an almost angelic figure who is all of the best aspects of their loved one, but without any of their less attractive features. More often than not, this comparison is conducted negatively: 'Ah, but my wife/husband/partner would never have done this. She/he was so kind, thoughtful and giving. I'll never meet anyone as good as her/him.'

While we would all like to remember our loved ones with the greatest of affection, it can be necessary, in order for the surviving partner to move on, for the ties with the first partner to be worked through and discussed in an objective manner by both parties in the early stages of a new relationship.

three

Facing death

The immediate formalities

The circumstances surrounding the death of someone vary enormously. Nevertheless, there are a number of formalities that have to be attended to right away by the bereaved or the bereaved's family.

If your loved one died suddenly at home the police may be obliged to take a statement, ask you to make a formal identification and satisfy themselves that there were no suspicious circumstances concerning the death. In some states in the USA, a doctor must be present to declare the person dead and state the cause of death. In other states and counties it is the duty of the coroner, or their appointed deputy, to identify the body formally. In hospital you may be asked by the doctors if you want a post-mortem examination, or autopsy. For some people, the thought of a post-mortem is horrific and they choose not to have one. Others want a definitive answer as to why their partner or family member died. You will not have much time to consider the options, but *do not* give your answer immediately. Take a few minutes to discuss your feelings with the doctors and, if possible, your family.

In some cases, including my own, where there is no known cause of death, you are not given a choice; the death is reported to the coroner or medical examiner who arranges a post-mortem. In Britain and Australia, a coroner is a doctor or lawyer responsible for investigating out-of-the-ordinary deaths. This is a role variously carried out by coroners, deputy coroners, medical examiners or deputy sheriffs in states and counties in the USA. These officials do not need your consent for an autopsy if the legal circumstances require one, but you may be able to have a doctor of your choice present during the operation. (For more information on the coroner's role, see page 46.)

If the cause of death is beyond doubt, the procedure is different from country to country and from state to state. In Britain, for example, the doctor will give you a Medical Certificate stating the cause. This will be in a sealed envelope, and addressed to the Registrar of Births, Deaths and Marriages. You will also be given a Formal Notice stating that the doctor has signed the Medical Certificate, and giving instructions on how to register the death. In Australia, it is the duty of the funeral director to gather information from you on the personal details of your loved one, including age, religion and the number of years they lived in all States and Territories, which is then passed on to the Registrar. You may also be asked, or express a wish, for the body or organs to be used for medical purposes.

Whatever the case, this intrusion by strangers so immediately after the first tidal wave of emotion following someone's death is deeply shocking. The same is true of the cold, formal wording of the paperwork. I vividly remember being handed the consent form for Shirin's post-mortem and signing it. There was a space beside where I had written my name with the words: 'Relationship to the Deceased'. I was brought up short for a moment, not realizing that Shirin had become 'the Deceased' and my relationship to her was no longer 'Husband', but 'Widower'.

You may also be asked to sign receipts for personal items, such as jewellery, which are removed from the body and returned to the next of kin soon after death.

If you are lucky enough to have your family around you they will provide welcome support at this trying time. Hospital staff, police and paramedics will all have had experience of death and will do all they can to help you. Talk to them, accept their condolences and kind words. They will mean them.

Telephoning friends and relations

The police or hospital staff may volunteer to call relations on your behalf. Remember that you are not obliged to call your friends and relatives immediately. I chose to wait until I had had a few hours to think and decide who to call and who I should visit in person to break the news. But it is a thankless task under any circumstances. I was fortunate in being able to share it with Shirin's family.

If you *do* want to call friends and relatives straight away try to remember the following points:

- **Write a few notes on what you intend to say** This will force you to gather your thoughts and make it easier for you to speak.

- **Keep it short** There will be plenty of time to talk in the days to come. Don't allow anyone (however well-intentioned) to upset you by saying how tragic and how sad it all is. You will need all your strength to get through the next few days. If you feel you are beginning to get flustered say that you have other calls to make and put the phone down.

- **Don't forget that people may be shocked** Ironically, you may find that you will have to assume the role of 'comforter'. Be prepared to console the people you call as well as tell them what has happened.

You will need to choose your words carefully to avoid any misunderstandings. I remember making my first call to Ruth, a friend that we were both particularly close to. I started off quite well. I told her that I was very sorry, but she had to prepare herself for some bad news. I then told her that we'd 'lost' Shirin. Ruth asked what I meant. I said: 'Shirin has passed away.'

It's probably better not to use euphemisms for death or dying because they are trivial, probably undignified and, by definition, avoid the issue. They also make it more difficult for the people you call to understand exactly what you mean and for them to accept the truth. On reflection, I perhaps should have said what had really happened: Shirin *died*. I might have added that Shirin didn't have a lingering death and that I would contact Ruth later about funeral arrangements. As it was I ended up upsetting myself, and both upsetting and confusing Ruth.

Of course, if you do not feel strong enough, let the police or hospital staff make a few of the most important calls. There is no shame in feeling unable to cope at this time. Your life has been shattered.

Viewing the body

If it is possible, the hospital staff will ask if you want to see the body. I can only speak from personal experience and say that I am extremely thankful that I chose to see Shirin after she'd died. I found it a strangely beautiful and moving experience. Her body had been moved into a room just off the Intensive Care Unit. The doctors and nurses had done an excellent job of making her look her best. In common with many people who see their loved ones in such circumstances, I thought she looked so much alive, but she was dead. I spent a short while with her mother, who later left so that I could have a last few minutes to say goodbye.

I did not realize at the time that this was a hugely important event. The most common initial reaction to the news of someone's death is disbelief. However, it is fundamental to the easing of grief to face up to and accept the reality that your loved one has died. Seeing Shirin's body in the hospital satisfied me that she *had* died. It wasn't a mistake. I was also relieved to see that she showed no signs of any pain or suffering.

My brother- and sister-in-law, who were also at the hospital, did not want to see Shirin's body. This was their own choice and I have never questioned it.

Later in the day

There will come a point when you will either have to leave the hospital or watch as the funeral directors take away the body. This is an experience that may seem almost absurd. I remember driving from the hospital back to the house with my brother-in-law. We hardly mentioned Shirin and mostly talked about a car he'd recently bought that he was having problems with. For the moment I had no more tears. I just felt totally exhausted.

There are two things you *must* remember to do at this point:

- **Eat** Even if you don't feel like it, have a simple meal or snack.

- **Rest** You might think that it's somehow wrong to rest after such a desperate event, but it's important to slow down. If you can, take a nap. If not, sit in a quiet room and talk to someone you know well about the way you feel; there will be plenty time to deal with funeral arrangements and financial and legal obligations later.

The first week

You will probably be too busy to think deeply about your grief in the first week. There is an enormous amount to do. Uppermost in people's minds at this time is the funeral. It provides a focus and purpose in the first days. Depending on the circumstances surrounding the death you may be able to proceed quite quickly with the funeral arrangements. You will be informed by hospital staff or the coroner when you are allowed to make contact with the funeral director. In my case I was not permitted to do so until the post-mortem had been carried out and the coroner was satisfied that my wife's death was due to natural causes that posed no threat to public health.

The coroner

In Britain, if the cause of death is not known or unexplained, the doctor may report the death to the coroner. Likewise, if your loved one died while under anaesthetic or during an operation or as a result of an accident, injury or industrial disease, the coroner may be involved. This is a sequence of events broadly similar to that in North America, Australia and New Zealand, but the categories of death leading to an investigation may vary. For example, in some US states, the coroner, or the official with equivalent powers, is required to take blood or other fluids after deaths following swimming, boating or vehicle accidents. These fluids are sent off to state laboratories for toxicological investigation. In many states the coroner, or the deputy coroner, may be asked to investigate a death believed to have been caused by starvation or alcoholism, or if Sudden Infant Death Syndrome is the suspected cause of death. In other states, all deaths in state mental health institutions are routinely dealt with by the coroner or county medical officer.

This complicates matters as these officials have the legal authority to retain the body until they are satisfied with the cause of death or until an inquiry has taken place. This is the case in Britain, where you cannot register the death until the coroner has certified the cause of death. However, if the coroner believes that a lengthy inquest has to be held, you may be given an Order for Burial or Certificate for Cremation so that the funeral can take place.

The inquest

An inquest, or coroner investigation as it's known in the US, is a public inquiry into the causes and circumstances of a death. It can involve relatives being asked questions as witnesses. In some cases you may be entitled to financial compensation as a result of industrial negligence or perhaps if the death was caused by a traffic accident.

In most cases, an inquest will be held if:

- the death was violent or unnatural

- the death resulted from an industrial accident

- the death occurred in prison

- the post mortem did not reveal an acceptable explanation of the cause of death

Once the inquest or investigation has been completed, the officials will allow the body to be released (if it has been removed for investigation) so the procedure can move forward.

Registering the death

It is a legal requirement in Britain that the death is registered at the local registry office within five days unless an inquiry leads to a delay. Either you or a member of the family can do this. It is important to bear in mind that although the death of your loved one may have been a shattering event to you personally, it is all fairly routine to the registrar. They deal in full names, dates of birth, usual addresses and causes of death. The language used is formal and heartbreakingly distant: 'deceased', 'widow' and 'widower'.

While the procedures in other countries vary, the formalities can be complex. In Britain for example, to register a death you need to take a number of certificates along with you including a Medical Certificate, and what is known as the Pink Form, which is issued by a coroner if the post-mortem revealed that the death was due to natural causes. Under different circumstances, such as registering the death of a stillborn child, different certificates are needed depending on whether a doctor or midwife was present at the birth.

In all cases, it may take some time for the registrar to process all the information. Remember that if you have to do this in person, it can be distressing. Ask if you need copies of the Death Certificate because you may be required to present a copy or send one to banks, government agencies or insurance companies when making changes to the names of accounts, claims, or asking for readjustment in payments (see section on Other bureaucracy, pp. 54–56).

The funeral

Arrangements

The funeral is immensely important because it brings people together in a public acknowledgement of the finality of death. It helps to reorient the bereaved into their new, and unwanted, social roles as well as demonstrating immediate and extended family cohesion. For many, a funeral is also a deeply sacred occasion. However, I will not offer detailed guidance on the different religious canons that you feel you are obliged to observe following a death. If you have strong religious convictions you will naturally contact your religious leader and discuss your requirements with him or her.

There are other considerations. If you have no strong feelings, and there is no will with instructions for how the funeral is to be conducted, you might feel torn between burial or cremation. It is important to realize, though, that you do not necessarily have free choice in this. No one can be cremated until the cause of death is definitely known. The coroner may refuse an application for cremation. Even then, the officials in a crematorium have the power to refuse a cremation. For example, if they find that the body has a pacemaker or other implant that should have been removed they will refuse the cremation as these devices can explode in the cremation chamber. Not surprisingly, there are numerous forms to be completed – five forms in Britain. This seems complex, but the funeral director and crematorium will normally be very efficient in taking care of things.

Greater practical difficulties tend to arise, however, when you or other members of the family have few, confused or no religious beliefs. Some people experience a sense of unease when faced with the prospect of a religious service when they and/or their loved one had no religious convictions. But it is still possible to have a service that does not clash with their, or your, beliefs, and still remains a spiritual event. An alternative to more convention-al services is to have a humanist one. For my own part, even though I do not have any religious beliefs, I chose not to have a humanist service because I was uncomfortable with the notion of Shirin being eulogized by someone, *anyone*, who wasn't known to either of us.

I recognize that I was very fortunate in having strength enough to be able to lead my wife's funeral service and give the main address. If you do not think that you are able to do this you could ask a close relative or friend to speak for you. For example, I asked Shirin's brother, Jim, to speak as well.

Whatever you decide, remember this:

- **Please yourself**   The service only needs to satisfy *you* and no-one else; how you choose to bury your loved one is up to you. This is not being selfish. You are right to put your own needs first, especially at this time.

- **Do what feels right**   Listen to any advice that other peo-ple may give you (or seek out the advice of people who have gone through the same experience), but only accept it if it feels right. If not, reject it. You do not need to justify your decisions to anyone. Don't feel that you are obliged to have hymns or readings from religious texts at the service even if it is held in a church or crematorium. If you have any favourite music that you want to have played as the mourners enter and leave then make a recording and arrange with the undertaker to have it played. Similarly, if you want a non-religious text, significant to you, read at the service then ask the person making the address to incorporate it into their speech. Remember that the funeral doesn't have to be a distressing few minutes of anguish and despair. There's nothing wrong with making a joke or two. It's better to recall the happy memories and bring a smile to the faces of the mourners than dwell on the obvious injustice and tragedy of death.

- **Thank the congregation** You and your family will have to face the distress, disbelief and confusion of friends and family at the funeral. Yet again you may find that you have to adopt the difficult, and seemingly unfair, role of comforter. Of course, you will also be upset, but I found that it helped to thank and accept the condolences of all the people who came to the crematorium directly before and after the service. Remember that many of them will have travelled miles to attend the funeral and pay their respects.

Expenses

Funerals are expensive. In addition to, perhaps, hiring a hearse and cars for the family, requesting an extravagant coffin and engaging the services of a religious representative, there are hidden related costs such as death notices that may need to be posted in local newspapers to inform anyone who, in the confusion, you forgot to tell. You might also want to view the body for one last time before the coffin lid is put on; this will mean extra work for the undertaker and consequently more expense for you. The cost of flowers, especially wreaths, can quickly mount up. These are issues that are worth lengthy consideration before you commit (and possibly burden) yourself with heavy funeral costs.

Here are a few points that might help in making your choices:

- The amount of money that you spend on the funeral is not necessarily a reflection of the amount of love you had for the person who died. Don't think you're being tight-fisted if you question the undertaker's initial estimate for the funeral costs. If you want a simple funeral (for whatever reason) then don't hesitate to ask the undertaker if he or she can find ways of reducing the costs.

- A coffin does not need to be ostentatious with expensive woods and heavy silver handles. The only legal requirement is that the coffin lid should have a plate on it with the name of the person who has died.

- Wreaths are of no value after the funeral; they are simply burnt. If you want to have flowers, order bouquets and other arrangements. They are more worthwhile because they can be delivered to a local hospital afterwards so that other people can enjoy them. The undertaker is usually very happy to arrange this for you. Of course, you can take them home with you. Asking friends to give a donation to a favourite charity is a good alternative to what many people believe is money wasted on flowers.

A word of warning. Most funeral directors provide a good service and are immensely supportive and discreet, but unfortunately there is a growing trend for some of them to regard funerals as straightforward business opportunities. A large percentage of funeral homes, graveyards and crematoriums, despite solid Victorian outward appearances, are in reality owned by multinational conglomerates whose representatives want to maximize profits. There is often a significant difference, for instance, between the cost of cremations in local government premises and those under private control.

The private companies are very successful because they are dealing with an extremely vulnerable and suggestible clientele who, quite naturally, want the best for their loved one. It's not unusual for the bereaved to be shown glossy catalogues of expensive coffins to choose from, or to be pressed to spend a great deal of money on gravestones or inscriptions in the chapel of rest. Sometimes salespeople will also strongly suggest that you take up an expensive 'pre-death' policy with the company so that you are 'free from worry' about your own funeral.

If you have *any* doubts at all about the service you are getting, go and see another funeral director. It seems obvious to say that you are not obliged to accept the services of the first funeral director you make contact with, but, of course, people under the extreme stress of bereavement don't think about value for money. So, if possible, ask someone you can trust, but who's perhaps a bit removed from the trauma of the death, to find a suitable funeral director on your behalf.

Another option would be to make sure that the funeral director is a member of a recognized professional body. In Britain this is the National Association of Funeral Directors (NAFD). In the US the national body is the National Funeral Directors Association (NFDA). Both the NAFD and NFDA have a code of practice that all members are expected to follow. For example, any NAFD member is required to give you a price list on request, and not include extra charges on any original written estimate without first consulting you. In the US it is the responsibility of the funeral director to review the cost of all the services and merchandise you decide on, such as embalming, dressing your loved one's hair for viewing, the choice of caskets, burial, entombment or cremation. Similarly, these organizations recommend that members agree to make appropriate reductions in the final bill if services of a basic funeral are not required, or to provide additional services to meet the needs of each family they serve. A case for a reduction would be in, say, the use of family as pall bearers instead of the funeral director's staff.

In Britain, the NAFD can deal with any complaint you have with your chosen funeral director if that funeral director is a member of the association. If the funeral director is not a member of a national body, consult local government officials about how to proceed with any complaint you may have.

Funeral reception

Your first inclination after the funeral may well be to go home, shut the door and refuse to see anyone ever again. Even the *idea* of having a reception for all the people who came to pay their respects at the funeral might be something you feel you just *couldn't* cope with. This is very understandable. After all, you've just said goodbye to someone very dear to you. So you might say to yourself: 'When I feel a bit better, when I'm not so tearful and full of grief, *that's* when I'll start meeting people again.'

Unfortunately, the danger in this is that not *until* you start meeting people, socializing and taking part in everyday life, will you ever begin to start feeling better. You might not want to have a large number of people around you so soon after such a sad occasion, but a reception is a practical first step back into 'normal' public life. When you play the part of host you are forced into using ritualized speeches and expressions in greeting everyone, taking their coats, making sure that all the guests have enough to eat and drink and that they have somewhere to sit. It's surprisingly easy, almost automatic. Most important of all, you will be among friends and family (rather than total strangers) who will be naturally sympathetic and full of understanding if, at times, you find it difficult to remain composed. These are small steps, but vital ones if you are to break a potential cycle of inertia in which making excuses not to do something becomes almost habitual.

I ended up enjoying the reception after Shirin's funeral. My mother-in-law and her friends between them were able to produce more than enough food and drink for the dozens of people who had attended. Some of them had come a long way and others I hadn't seen for years. Apart from an initial few minutes of tension when no-one wanted to say anything for fear of saying the wrong thing, there was a lot of laughter and I heard some very enter-taining stories about Shirin (some for the first time) as well as sharing a few tears. I found great relief in being able to enjoy good company for a few hours. I had the chance to reminisce about the precious good times that I had had with her and the fun that she'd had with her friends before I'd met her.

There is, of course, an alternative to having a reception and that is to stay at home all alone and be miserable for hours, but I don't recommend it.

Other bureaucracy

I probably found it a relatively simple and straightforward process to register Shirin's death because I knew that the registrar was someone who was accustomed to death. It's part of his or her job. The formality of the setting and the language are all designed to make the procedure as easy and as smooth as possible. Similarly, lawyers are familiar with the distress of relatives who have to go to attend the reading of the will. However, I found it much more dif-ficult to face anonymous bank and building society tellers, post office workers and the receptionists at the local health clinic.

If you had a joint bank, building society, or other financial account with your partner, you will need to have the name of the account changed. If your partner had a bank account in their own name then you will have to start proceedings in order to release the money. You may be entitled to insurance benefits or an increased pension. Stocks and bonds need to be released and dis-tributed according to your loved one's wishes in the will (if there is one). In Britain, you may also need to return Premium Bonds, which means a trip to the post office to collect the relevant form, or have your mortgage reassessed. You will need to contact car and property insurance companies if any insurance was taken out in your loved one's name. The same is true of gas, electricity and telephone services. Of course, the local council or municipality may have to be told if any benefits or taxes were received or owed in the household.

It doesn't end there. You also have to return any driving licenses to the relevant authority, send passports back to the nearest agency for cancellation, hand over medical papers to your local clinic or hospital authorities, send local government documents, library cards, travel season tickets and any membership cards back to relevant offices with a note of explanation, and a claim for refund if appropriate.

These encounters I found to be very stressful and intense. Bank tellers and other staff who deal with the public are much more used to giving a cheery 'good morning!' and offering a smile, if you're lucky, before attending to the customer. In my experience, they are much less good at handling delicate situations that are more out of the ordinary. A lot depends, of course, on the sympathetic nature and social skills of the individual who is across the counter.

These steps will help reduce the stresses involved in completing these tasks:

- **Prioritize**   Write down a list of all of the institutions and agencies that you need to visit and put them in order of priority. Visit the most important first.

- **Make lists**   Find out what documents you'll need to take with you. These might include birth, marriage and death certificates as well as insurance and pension policies, medical cards, etc.

- **Arrange a meeting**   Try not to visit 'cold'. If possible, telephone and arrange a time to meet a specific named individual to complete the paperwork. Ask the person you've telephoned if there is a private room you can use for the interview; the last thing you'll want is to is conduct your business in public. Everybody will do all they can to accommodate you.

- **Take some support** It will help if you take a calm and unflappable friend or relative along with you to give you support, and help if you find it difficult to complete the paperwork.

The will

Viewed objectively, a will is nothing more than a legal document that details who is to benefit from someone's material and financial assets now that they are dead. It may or may not have been drawn up with the help and advice of a lawyer (it is possible in some countries and states to write a will without the help of a lawyer or attorney). When signed, witnessed and completed according to all legal requirements, it is a binding set of instructions regarding what is to be done with business interests and trust funds, and how assets are to be distributed amongst members of the family, friends and charities. Some wills are quite complex, but others are relatively straightforward. It all depends on the size and cohesion of the family, the total assets, and special interests and wishes of the person who died.

In Britain, the will's instructions are carried out by an individual known as an executor, who will have been nominated by the person who wrote the will. An executor cannot be a beneficiary of the will.

The document itself is often held by a lawyer or attorney for safekeeping, but may also have been deposited in a bank. If you're not sure of the existence of a will, these are the first places to look for one. And if it's not there or among any other personal papers, then it's more than likely that they died *intestate*, that is without leaving a will. In such a case, nearest relatives benefit from the total assets up to a certain point determined by legislation, after which the taxman takes a share.

Of course, to the bereaved a will isn't just words on paper expressing the final wishes of a loved one. It has greater significance. It's not just a question of money, clothes, books, pictures or jewellery; a will is often seen as a material expression of a beneficiary's personal worth and value in the eyes of their loved one. After all, isn't a will a *final* will and testament? And so when some other member of the family is given something that by rights you think *you* should have received, it can lead to acrimony, bitterness and resentment.

For these reasons, the reading of a will can be a stressful event that sometimes adds to pre-existing family tensions. The contents can be a disappointment and it's quite possible that you may have good reason to feel hard done by. You might feel that you have been snubbed in the worst kind of way by someone you thought loved you dearly. You may feel that you have been cut off from an inheritance which to others might seem trivial, but to you is highly significant.

However, even though we tend to view wills as carefully considered evaluations by a loved one, it's important to keep in mind that they are not necessarily representative of your loved one's thoughts at the moment when they died. They may not even be representative of their thoughts a month or even a week before they died. They are merely a reflection of what they were thinking at the time they wrote it. Try to put any anger you feel in perspective.

Letters of condolence

Very soon after the death of your loved one you will start to receive dozens of letters, cards and bouquets of flowers from all sorts of people. They will be from relatives, close friends, workmates and acquaintances you perhaps thought didn't care that much. They will probably vary in style from one or two lines expressing condolences in a rather stiff and formal manner to intensely personal declarations of sympathy and support.

Some people are better at writing letters than others, but it is important to remember that even though some people fumble for words and use ritualized expressions such as 'words are use-less . . . I don't know what to say . . . I wish there was something I could do', *all* of the people you get letters and cards from are try-ing to do their best to help and to wish you well.

Still, there is a possibility that there will be letters from people that will upset you. I particularly remember getting one from a work colleague who started with: 'Hiya man! How's it goin'?' I was stunned by the inappropriate tone; the crassness of the ques-tion astounded me. I was furious because I thought he belittled my circumstances. Of course, that wasn't his intention. He gen-uinely wanted to help and thought (wrongly) that I perhaps need-ed 'jollying along'.

Other people might slip in one or two phrases referring to the death of your loved one in an otherwise 'normal' letter. This hurts because it seems as though it's a deliberate sleight. The reality is different. Anyone who has *not* gone through the experience of loss finds it hard to empathize with the bereaved, and their lack of understanding is clear in the obvious awkwardness of their approach. But behind the awkwardness are genuine feelings.

Helpful advice

I found strength and comfort through reading all of the letters of support that I received, but there was a category of letter that stood out from the rest. These were the letters from people who had gone through the same experience as me. In addition to offers of sympathy they also gave practical advice on how to deal with the agonies of the moment.

Here is a compilation of some of their recommendations:

- **What has happened has happened** Accept it. This may seem almost callous, but you have no choice except to adopt a pragmatic approach, and acknowledge the inevitable fact of the death of your loved one. The longer you deny they are gone, the longer it will take you to start to heal.

- **Be kind to yourself** Do what *you* want and what *you* need. Don't let *anyone*, however well-intentioned, bully you into making decisions that don't seem right to you. (I remember my boss phoning me up quite soon after Shirin's funeral asking me when I was going to go back to work. The answer to that question, and any other of that type, is: 'When I'm ready.')

- **Be busy** Take on as much work as you feel you are able to handle. If you have no job, try and occupy yourself with every-day tasks, go to libraries, exhibitions or take long walks. If you can, take on a regular voluntary job. Try to meet people. Although this is very difficult at first, the sooner you start to begin to reorient your life the sooner your confidence will return.

- **Be patient** Don't make any major decisions about your life for maybe a year, or even more. The great temptation is to *do something*, draw a line and begin again. You might think about leaving the house or flat you were living in, changing your job or settling down with a new partner. There's no need to hurry; let the momentum of life carry you along until you are a little bit stronger and ready to make good, considered choices.

- **Have no regrets** You loved and you were loved. Don't worry yourself with what arguments you had in the past or what plans you had for the future. Remember the past, but don't live by it.

- **Accept the future** Prepare to accept that the direction of your life will change. Although you may not be able to (or per-haps want to) anticipate it, there will be new opportunities *because* of what has happened rather than in spite of it.

If you are grieving for a parent who has died after a long and full life, it is possible to find some comfort in knowing that their death, before yours, is the 'natural' and inevitable order of things. It is very much harder if you have lost a child, or a partner at a young age. No-one expects to be present at the funeral of their own child. I certainly did not expect to become a widower at the age of thirty-five. The sense of injustice and tragedy is overwhelming.

The only way that I felt able to overcome these feelings of injustice was to alter my whole attitude to what had happened. I did this with help from a letter I received from an acquaintance of my mother-in-law's, whose son had died at the age of forty-two. She said that it didn't help to dwell on the obvious tragedy of a young life lost. It was more fitting and healthier to think in terms of a life that was complete rather than cruelly cut short. This allowed me to look beyond the immediate sorrowful circumstances of Shirin's death and see what we'd meant to each other, what we'd enjoyed together and what we'd achieved together.

After you've read the letters and cards that you receive and accepted all of the flowers that come, you have to make a decision as to whether you are going to write back in acknowledgement and thank all of the people who sent them.

The easiest option is not to write; nobody really expects a reply. However, I found it very comforting to take the opportunity to thank everyone for the trouble and time they had taken in giving their support. Part of my letters included a few paragraphs on Shirin and what she meant to me. I spent some time thinking about her qualities and of the happy times that we'd had together before I put pen to paper and found that, even though it was a very distressing process because it was so close to the event, I was able to begin to develop a more positive outlook on my situation.

section two
Rebuilding your Life

At first when you are bereaved, life might appear empty and without reason. In the case of a partner dying, all the plans you made together now have no point, and confidence in yourself and others will probably be at an all-time low. The intensity of these feelings will depend on how much you relied on your partner for emotional support, help, advice, fun, friendship and love. Almost certainly your anxiety levels will be heightened, and your ability to relax and to make decisions diminished. You probably won't feel like going out to work or to meet people in social situations. In fact, you may feel suspicious of others' motives when they offer help and advice.

These symptoms of grief can be viewed from two key perspectives. For example, the loss of someone dear inevitably involves philosophical questions relating to the meaning of life, and an intense personalization of the 'purpose' of death. This often prompts feelings of unreality about life, of aloneness and dread. Similarly, the death of a loved one can lead to an exploration of spiritual issues. If you believe in an afterlife you may feel comfort in knowing that your loved one has found peace, and that you will be reunited after death.

However, death can also shake belief, and you might be experiencing guilt at doubting the existence of a god if your loved one died violently or young. In the circumstances of a confused, or non-existent, spiritual base to someone who has been bereaved, it is likely that in a deeper sense there will be feelings of desolation, and of there being no meaning to life. For my own part, I occasionally felt emptiness and even envy of those who *did* have faith to comfort them and give them hope.

Symptoms of grief can also be seen as exerting psychological and physical demands on the bereaved. It's quite common to see images of your loved one in an almost hallucinatory fashion. Depression, anger and anxiety can make it difficult to sleep. It's not unusual for the recently bereaved to suffer nausea, palpitations, headaches or even develop symptoms similar to an illness that might have led to the death of their loved one. There is an increased risk of becoming susceptible to disease, particularly if eating habits are changed; it's very easy to skip meals or not bother exercising at times of great stress.

You may have to tackle some or all of these problems if you are going to make an effective recovery from the shock of separation. The aim of the following chapters, first outlined to me by Dr Robert Burns, an Australian-based educational psychologist, is to empower you with the key skills for increasing your physical and mental strength so that you can once again begin to enjoy life. These skills comprise: confidence-building, relaxation skills, interpersonal skills, decision-making skills and the expertise necessary for living a healthier life.

four

Confidence-building

The death of someone close to you will bring about a diminution in your feelings of confidence and self-worth. You may find that the 'inner voice' within you (and within *all* of us) will start to try to persuade you that you are 'worthless' without your partner, that you're 'not competent enough' to tackle the challenges that lie ahead. If you listen to this silver-tongued inner voice you will soon find yourself believing that you *are* worthless and incompetent and your inability to face these challenges will become a self-fulfilling prophecy. It may be tempting to believe that you 'can't cope', but, apart from being untrue, it's like starting a race carrying a couple of wet sandbags – you're bound to lose.

Self-worth

Instead of encouraging a negative internal monologue, the first step towards increased confidence is to develop a stronger sense of self-worth. Self-worth consists of a number of intermeshed elements including:

- your *emotional* self-worth, i.e. the emotions that you consider to be characteristic of you

- your *personal* self-worth, i.e. how you perceive yourself at this moment

- your *social* self-worth, i.e. how you perceive others think of you

- your *intellectual* self-worth, i.e. how 'clever' you perceive yourself to be

- your *physical* self-worth, i.e. how healthy and attractive you feel you are

It is highly likely that many, if not all, of these elements will have been severely shaken by the ordeal of bereavement. For example, under normal circumstances you might consider yourself to be very positive emotionally. You might think of yourself as a happy, contented and loving person and so the negative emotions of anger, dread, guilt and sadness that are commonly associated with bereavement could be very upsetting. You might be tempted to hide or deny these negative feelings, which in turn could lead to greater stresses and consequent emotional problems later on.

A more positive approach would be to be open and express these negative feelings despite your misgivings. Moreover, you are *entitled* to express your feelings of pain and sadness. It is entirely appropriate under the circumstances.

Similarly, you might sense a shift in your feelings of personal self-worth. The death of someone close to you can feel as though part of you has been physically ripped out of you and, on an emotional level, it may seem as though a greater part of your reason for living has been taken away. Perhaps, if your son or daughter has died, you may feel as if you have somehow 'failed' as a parent even though you know that rationally you are in no sense culpable.

Very negative changes can also occur in your sense of social self-worth when someone close to you dies. Some people avoid social situations where they know that they will meet someone who's recently been bereaved and it's possible you might take on board a sense of being a social outcast. You might also believe that as a widow or widower you could be perceived as a threat to the husband or wife of couples you know. In addition, when you begin to meet new people again and possibly someone you might want to know more intimately, you might feel socially inept. This would be especially true if you believe you're 'out of practice' in getting to know other people.

On an intellectual level you may feel yourself challenged, if not incapable, of tasks that others find very ordinary. For example, Shirin took responsibility for all of our joint bank accounts, building society savings, premium bonds and insurance policies. She paid all credit card, electricity and gas bills. I had very little idea of our assets and initially experienced a flood of panic at my incompetence when I had to fill out my first credit-card demand. If you find yourself in situations where you feel that you may show yourself up intellectually, you will inevitably feel stress. On a mundane level this might be at a party where you feel you are expected to keep up a constant line in witty banter. If you're tackling higher qualifications or in a job where you have to make rational decisions you might miss the chats you had with your partner when you were dealing with a knotty intellectual problem and think that, perhaps, you won't be able to do your best without them. It's also possible that your partner may have constantly told you that you were 'stupid' and you might have ended up believing him or her.

Our sense of physical self-worth is often of great importance to us. We are always with our body and it's possibly true to say that most of us would want to change it in some way. Some people think that they are too short or too tall or too fat or too thin. Others think that even total strangers focus on minor imperfections like a slightly protruding ear or an insignificant birthmark.

If we experience the death of a partner these 'imperfections' almost inevitably seem to become exaggerated. After all, your partner (more or less) accepted your changing body over the years. If, like many people, you have let yourself go during the

time you were together with your partner you will have further
reason to have negative thoughts about your body image: are you
still attractive enough to find another partner? Are people so put
off by what they see that they don't want to get to know you
better?

The most simple and effective way of improving your physical
self-worth is to follow a sensible diet and exercise programme (see
Chapter 8). This has additional side benefits of adding an extra
support structure to your life and significantly reducing stress
through the release of natural chemical endorphins.

Self-evaluation

An improved level of self-worth will significantly reduce the levels
of anxiety that you will be feeling after the death of your loved
one. To do this you will need to discover (or even rediscover) your
strengths and weaknesses. Once you know these you will be able
to play to them and be more confident and resilient in facing the
daunting challenges of the future.

Essentially, you will have to evaluate your own abilities and
skills. Self-evaluation is not always easy and there are a number of
very important points that you should remember when you sit
down and do it:

- **Be honest with yourself**   You will only defeat the purpose of the exercise if you try and kid yourself that you have
  qualities that you would *like* to have rather than acknowledge
  the ones you possess.

- **Don't compare yourself with others**   When we compare ourselves with other people we seem to have a natural
  tendency to highlight *their* strengths while putting ourselves
  down. Remember this is *self*-evaluation.

- **Concentrate on the positive aspects of your self-
  worth**   Anyone can run themselves down. If you start to

dwell on the weaker parts of your total self then you will begin to think of yourself as a failure and you will be defeated almost as soon as you've begun.

Self-evaluation activity

The following activity is designed to help you in thinking about your positive qualities and your abilities and skills in all aspects of your total self. Give yourself time to think before completing these tasks:

Positive personal and emotional qualities

1. Write down five key positive qualities that you believe constitute your personal and emotional character. You might, for example, consider yourself to be honest, trustworthy or reliable.

2. Underneath each quality write a short narrative of an occasion when you were, say, conscientious, generous or decisive. It is important to remember that although you may feel a little disoriented at present there was a time when you proved your competence. And you *will* be competent again.

Positive social skills

1. Write down details of five separate occasions when you demonstrated your social ability. For example, times when you felt particularly good about getting on with and getting to know other people, helping others when they were in trouble or listening and showing an interest in what other people said or did.

2. Look at what you have written. Are there any common features that occur in these incidents? What features and qualities do you think make you good at forming relationships and interacting with others?

Positive intellectual abilities

1. Think of five situations in which you thought through a problem to a successful conclusion. Perhaps you particularly remember becoming involved in and stimulated by an academic task or writing and delivering an effective speech. Maybe you were asked to design a programme or asked to organize an event that went very well.

2. Write down your thoughts on these achievements. What features of your achievements do you think could be applied to your present situation?

Positive practical skills and artistic abilities

1. Write a list of all the skills and artistic abilities you possess. You might be good at repairing cars or electronic equipment or making things from bits and pieces you find round the house. You might be a good cook, be able to play a musical instrument, paint, draw or act.

2. Think about how you can use these skills and abilities in the coming weeks and months to keep busy, meet people and keep depression at bay.

Positive physical abilities

1. Make a list of physical activities you enjoy participating in. Are you good at a particular sport? Do you enjoy walking in the hills, jogging or swimming? You might have played sport to a high level. This is something you can be justifiably proud of.

2. Think about how you can use these activities to add enjoyment and structure to your life. You may feel it's not 'right' to enjoy life when something so devastating has happened, but it is essential to realize that even though a vital part of your life has gone you are still entitled to enjoy yourself; you should not feel guilty about getting out and having fun.

Building positive thought

At the same time that you are trying to rebuild your feelings of self-worth, you should also try to develop constructive attitudes towards yourself, your surroundings and circumstances. In this way you will avoid developing habits and behaviours that encourage you to play the role of victim.

Playing victim isn't feeling the crushing pain of loss, it's assuming a negative role long after your loved one's death. It is almost seductive to play victim when someone close to you has died. It's easy to say: 'How can this have happened to *me*? I just *can't* cope. I *can't* go on. There's *no* hope!' and pass it off as a justifiable lament. However, a destructive inner monologue of this type can easily stimulate self-perpetuating, self-defeating apathy full of 'if-only' wishful thinking. Allowing yourself to become upset and tormenting yourself about what you cannot change will bring you no benefits.

The only payoff from sustained self-indulgent 'victim' behaviour is tension, depression and misery. If one thing is absolutely certain, it isn't *just* the dreadful circumstances of death and separation that makes bereavement so difficult to bear, it's the attitude we take towards it. At first despair and a feeling of hopelessness are very understandable and to be expected. However, after a while when you feel a little calmer and more rational, you can choose either to nod your head, accept what has happened (however devastating) and develop a positive attitude, or to behave as though you're the only person in the world who's suffering – at least that's the way it'll appear to other people.

There are several ways in which you can counter the negative thinking that is so often part and parcel of the bereavement process. They include the following techniques: thought-stopping, creating constructive inner monologues, promoting positive addiction and developing a positive support system.

Thought-stopping

It is almost inevitable that at times you will find yourself slipping into a negative internal monologue. One way of preventing this from happening is to make a conscious effort to 'stop' yourself from thinking such thoughts. A proven method is thought-stopping. A typical thought-stopping procedure is outlined below:

1. When you next start brooding on your situation externalize what you are thinking. Say what you are thinking out loud.

2. Interrupt these negative thoughts by saying **'STOP'** loudly.

3. Repeat this process five times.

4. Repeat the process again, but say 'stop' to yourself quietly under your breath.

5. On the final repetition say 'stop' in your head. I have found that imagining the words being crossed out on a page as I say the final 'stop' helps as a symbolic closure of the thoughts.

This procedure can easily be used when you are alone (when most of these negative thoughts happen). It is important to realize that it is a procedure that should be repeated frequently so that it occurs almost automatically and shuts off the negative feelings, thoughts and emotions before they take a hold.

Constructive inner monologues

We talk to ourselves all the time, often without realizing it. We normally only become conscious of it when we are faced with problems and stressful situations. It is at these times that our internal monologues become negative. When someone has suffered a bereavement, they have such thoughts as: 'I *can't* cope without him . . .', 'If *only* she hadn't died . . .' or 'What will I do . . . ?'

This type of thought can be replaced with positive self-instruction. It is not just a question of word substitution or semantics. Just as you can talk yourself into despair and failure, it is possible to talk yourself into contentment and success.

- 'I can't' has to be replaced with 'I can'. You may not necessarily completely believe that you *can* get through what you may feel is the greatest ordeal of your life, but you *will* get through it and the process will be speeded up considerably if you start to think positively. Instead of thinking: 'I can't', think 'I can cope without them. I managed before and I will again.'

- All sentiments prefaced with 'if only' are exercises in futility. The tragic fact is that your loved one *has* gone and that you *have* to accept it. These statements should be replaced with 'I accept that she/he has died and that my life has changed. I have to look to the future.'

- 'What will I do . . . ?' reflects the despair of the recently bereaved. It would probably be unnatural if you did not have any anxiety for the future. However, you will serve yourself better if you replace these words with 'I will' and 'I know that I can get my life together again. I know it will be difficult, but I will do it.'

Of these three examples, it is perhaps the negative thoughts in 'What will I do?' which are the most difficult to counter. It is probably true to say that, at first, most people whose partner or child has died find it difficult, if not impossible, to think about the future. A day at a time is about as much as they can handle. Anything more is too traumatic. This feeling can persist for weeks, if not months.

Here is a constructive inner monologue that is designed for use on a day-to-day basis:

Today I'll try and adjust to my circumstances. I won't think 'if only' thoughts.
Today I'll strengthen my mind with positive thoughts. I'll focus on what gives me comfort and hope.
Today I'll try to be more sociable. I'll present myself in my best light.
Today I'll look after my body. I'll eat well and do some exercise.
Today I'll put some time aside to relax and let go of my anxieties.
Today I'll not be afraid to be happy.

The essential difference between negative and positive internal monologues is that the former normally occur as reactions to an event or events while the latter are devices intended to deflect negative thoughts in advance or in the midst of stress. One way in which you can fully prepare is by writing a personal script of how you will react to an event before it happens. The sequence of steps in writing a personal script of this type is as follows:

1. **Think about an event**   Recall an incident that happened very soon after your loved one died which involved your reacting in a negative way. This could entail negative thoughts when you started meeting people after the funeral, what you said to someone when they (inadvertently) said something to upset you, or perhaps an incident that happened when you had to do something on your own that your partner normally did.

2. **Become aware**   Think about the nature and substance of your thoughts. Write down the thoughts you had before, during and after this incident.

3. **Analyse what you have written**   Which of these thoughts were negative and self-defeating? Were your thoughts based on fact or potentially self-centred? When did these thoughts occur? Was it before, during or after the incident?

4. **Review your analysis** Was there anything that you could have said or thought that might have been more useful at that time or in a similar situation in the future?

5. **Reframe your attitude** Imagine yourself in this same situation. Re-enact the scene using the positive thoughts and feelings that you have constructed. Internalize these thoughts and feelings, and apply what you have learnt to the situation as it occurs.

Positive addiction

One way of overcoming a reluctance to be positive after the shattering event of death is to find an activity so divorced from your sad circumstances that you can do it without feeling guilt. The idea behind this is simple. If you can become positively addicted to an activity in one area of your life, realize that it is worthwhile and that it generates strong and beneficial differences in your life, you can use this knowledge and experience to effect positive change in other areas of your life.

Positive addiction is the start of a process through which someone who has suffered a bereavement should be able to rediscover that life *is* worth living when seemingly everything of value has been so cruelly taken away. The easiest activities to become positively addicted to are those that satisfy the following criteria:

- they take about one hour of your time

- they require little or no mental effort

- they can be done alone

- they are non-competitive

- they are not open to critical observation

- they have physical, metaphysical or intellectual value

- they will bring about a degree of positive improvement for the person doing them

The sorts of activities that fulfil these critereria are those that probably have a mechanical and monotonous quality to them such as gentle jogging, meditating or walking in the countryside or park – all of which promote a feeling of well-being because of their soothing effect. It is believed that people who become positively addicted to an activity that they choose to do on a regular basis develop the ability to deal more effectively with stress than those who do not.

Developing a support system

The death of someone close to you causes emptiness and imbalance in your life. For many people the pain of separation almost crushes them, so desperate is their loss. In the case of a long-standing relationship, over time you may have unconsciously excluded people from your life together, thus increasing stress and feelings of isolation and loneliness now that your partner is no longer there.

There are two ways of developing a support system outlined below. The first of these looks at how you might restructure your whole life after a death. The second looks at support structures from the perspective of people who might be helpful in seeing you through stressful times. Although these sections take the loss of a partner as their starting point, the sources of support are relevant for any bereaved person in need of support.

Whole life support

It is not unusual for partners of long standing to rely so much on each other that when one dies the other is left with an enormous hole in their life. Dr Susan Jeffers, a Californian psychologist, has used the following illustration to demonstrate this:

Whole life with partner   Whole life without partner

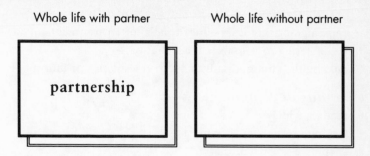

partnership

While this might seem an extreme and perhaps simplistic example, it is possibly not too far from the truth, or from what the bereaved *perceives* to be the truth, of the situation.

It doesn't have to be this way after the death of a loved one. It is possible to construct a fuller and more dynamic whole life support structure that draws you into activities with other people and deflects depression and stress. Below are eight categories with examples that could be added to a whole life support structure:

Leisure

- going to a film or the theatre
- going to a sports event
- going to a party
- going out for a meal or a drink with friends
- collecting something that interests you
- playing chess, bridge, draughts, scrabble or board games with friends
- developing an interest in photography, gardening or DIY

Culture

- going to a concert or a play
- going to a museum or art gallery
- going to a lecture or workshop of a cultural nature
- joining a theatre group
- listening to your favourite music

Contributing to your local community
- campaigning on local political, social or environmental issues
- volunteering to help for a local charity
- helping the young, disadvantaged, elderly, sick or infirm

Personal development
- reading widely
- writing prose, poems or music
- keeping a journal or diary
- practising a musical instrument for your own pleasure

Physical activity
- running or jogging
- joining a sports club or gym
- going fishing
- getting involved in water sports

Outdoor life
- going hill-walking or mountain-climbing
- going on picnics or camping
- developing an active interest in bird- or animal-watching
- taking an interest in plants and plant life
- getting involved in outward bound centres

Spending money
- going to auctions or sales
- buying something special for yourself
- buying something special for someone else
- buying a piece of artwork or a picture that you like
- choosing to contribute to a favourite charity

Work, family and friends
- building a positive work relationship with co-workers
- trying to see others' point of view
- trying to compromise and negotiate any differences between you
- being genuine in your dealings with others

All of these areas and categories can be built into your life and can help in combating the sense of isolation that bereavement can bring. The illustration below shows at a glance that even though there is a gaping hole representing the death of your loved one, there is still enough to support you while you begin to recover. This more active existence should give a little more meaning to your life as a whole which, of course, has suffered a traumatic reverse.

Whole life without partner

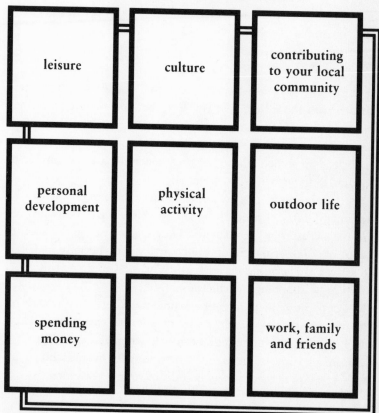

Of course, these categories and examples do not exhaust the possible permutations. You might want to try and add to them or devise categories of your own that suit your tastes. You don't have to do everything at once, you can choose to do one of these a day or certain of them regularly once a week. To do them often and regularly is the important thing.

It is quite likely, however, that a person who has suffered a bereavement will feel guilt at engaging in activities that involve an element of fun and enjoyment. It is *essential* to remember that you are entitled to be happy and to enjoy yourself; if you have fun this does *not* mean that you have forgotten that your loved one is gone and that you loved them or are, somehow, showing disrespect for their memory.

Personal support

It is possible that you are convinced that you shouldn't burden anyone with the misery that you feel, that you should keep your pain to yourself. You are mistaken. We all have the right to feel and express pain, and to ask for help and support. This is especially true for someone who has been bereaved. It can be difficult, though, to know where to ask for support.

Relatives and friends are not necessarily the best people to ask. You might know of people who are good in a crisis, but who you are not necessarily friends with. They might also be the sort of people that in normal circumstances irritate you because they like to ask searching questions such as: 'Why are you doing this . . . ? What are you hoping to achieve . . . ?'

Alternatively, there might be people you know, even friends of friends, who have experienced a bereavement themselves. They will have vital information that can help you. Seek them out.

Here are some of the main characteristics of people who could be 'helpers' over the first few months of your bereavement:

- **They are people who offer their help and support –
  and *mean* it**   Remember that 'If there's anything I can do, just ask' is a ritualized expression that people use when someone has been bereaved. Some people might mean it when they

say it, but the reality is that over time they will be less and less willing to give up their time for you. When you realize that they are no longer willing to help it will hurt. Be prepared for this.

- **You can trust them not to betray your confidences**
  You may feel almost impelled to divulge intensely personal information immediately after the death of your loved one. This could be because you feel guilt at, perhaps, having done something that you are ashamed of in the relationship you had with your partner. Naturally, you would not want that information to become common knowledge.

- **They have also gone through the process of bereavement** When Shirin died, the most valuable advice I received was from three people who had also lost people close to them. One of them I had known as a friend, a second I had known as a colleague, but the third I only knew through a friend of a friend from my days at university. It didn't matter that I knew one of them well and the others hardly at all, there was a common bond in our shared experiences.

- **You believe that what they have to say or what they will do will have a positive impact on the way you are behaving or thinking** This means they could be people who give crucial direction to your life or, equally, people who just make you feel good about yourself and who you can be totally yourself with.

It can be difficult to determine the best candidates from whom you should accept offers of help and support. One way is to complete the following exercise, which is designed to help you examine and become aware of the amount of trust you invest in, and support you believe you receive from, groups of people you are likely to interact with in normal everyday life.

Look at the chart below. One column is labelled 'Trust' and the other 'Support'. Each column is divided into three classifications of people you are most likely to interact with on a day-to-day level: co-workers family, friends.

In the spaces below each classification write down the names, in rank order, of the three people you think you can trust and expect support from.

Trust ▭   ## Support ▭

Co-workers

1. _____

2. _____

3. _____

Co-workers

1. _____

2. _____

3. _____

Family

1. _____

2. _____

3. _____

Family

1. _____

2. _____

3. _____

Friends

1. _____

2. _____

3. _____

Friends

1. _____

2. _____

3. _____

Look at the completed chart and think about these questions:

1.   Did any of your selections surprise you? Why?

2. Is there any similarity between those people you trust and those people that offer you support?

3. Did you find out that your needs in one area were not being met?

4. Did the same few people turn up in the first column of each category?

If you believe that either your trust or support system is incomplete then you should try to look around for likely people who could help you. Similarly, if there seem to be only one or two people who feature prominently in your completed chart, then you might want to consider expanding your circle of helpers. After all, these people might not always be about. They might move or become involved in activities that restrict their social life.

five

Relaxation and meditation techniques

One of the greatest problems with bereavement is the seeming overload of stress. So much needs to be done all at once. This stress will be manifested in some form or another, whether through anger, tension or loss of sleep. The aim of this chapter is to provide examples of healthy and beneficial ways of dealing with it through different relaxation techniques. After experimenting with these and finding those that you like, you will find, if you persevere, that you'll be able to go on and develop an almost automatic positive response to stress in all its forms.

There are, of course, other ways of relieving stress and finding comfort that you might be tempted to try. Raiding the fridge and eating the contents is one way. Another is to drink the best part of a bottle of whisky or vodka. You might also want to up your nicotine levels or pop a few anti-depressants: 'Just to help me through . . .' While any of these methods will temporarily relieve the symptoms of stress, they won't help you in the long run. Indeed, they will almost certainly add to your stress levels by ruining your health and by distorting your body image and feelings of self-worth.

The attraction of these self-destructive approaches to stress management is that they are so easy to do. It requires no special skill to open a bottle of whisky or to allow yourself to float in a drug-induced haze, whereas a programme of relaxation is a physical skill that requires time, effort and discipline. However, the benefits of learning how to relax at a time like this are worth it. They include a decrease in:

- **Tension** Bereavement almost inevitably brings about stresses that are physical. Some relaxation techniques can help specifically in reducing stress-related muscular tension and other problems such as tension headaches, high blood pressure and an abnormally high heart rate.

- **Depression and anxiety** Relaxation skills will help promote feelings of well-being. You may have found that since the death of your loved one you have become more irritable and consequently much more difficult to get along with. By relaxing you will be able to release much of the negative emotional energy that has built up within you and, at the same time, promote a more positive framework for interacting with others.

They also include an increase in:

- **Energy** Tension and anxiety sap energy levels. You might have found yourself lying awake at night not resting properly because you are worrying about what (in reality) may be trivial, but because of your heightened state of mental arousal you have been unable to think rationally. In addition, the physical stresses that you may have been experiencing may have seriously depleted your energy reserves. By being able to relax you will be able to conserve these reserves.

- **Self-worth** Relaxation can be a form of conscious self-control. It is possible to learn to become aware of your mind-and-body state and control it. When you are able to do this you will find that your confidence levels are increased and your feelings of self-worth are enhanced.

Learning and practising a relaxation technique require a fairly high level of commitment and for this reason many people are reluctant to start and maintain one. There are other problems and pretexts for not beginning or carrying on, including lack of time or a quiet space, or too many interruptions. Some people might feel guilty at apparently just sitting around wasting time so soon after their loved one has died when so many material things need to be attended to. Others might be afraid that they will be laughed at by family or friends. After all, there are many negative connotations associated with some forms of relaxation, meditation being one example. It is not unusual for people to be worried about becoming detached from reality, or losing control of themselves, or to be afraid that their minds will become sluggish and slow over time.

However, research into the experience and results of relaxation techniques does not appear to bear any of these fears out. Many of the minor negative consequences of relaxation can be put down to a lack of adequate preparation, or an over-reaction to some of the physical problems that can be a natural result of learning to relax. In some techniques of relaxation, for instance, the muscles are consciously tensed and then relaxed which, at first, can sometimes result in muscle cramps. Similarly, tension may be released through an involuntary jerking of the arms and legs. It's also possible that when you begin you will find it difficult to maintain a comfortable position to relax in.

Starting a relaxation programme

There are two main aims in your pursuing a relaxation programme. The first is to find the natural state of mind that enables you effectively to control and relieve the symptoms of stress. This can be achieved through one or more different relaxation techniques. The second is to transfer those feelings of relaxation to the context of stresses built up after bereavement.

There are some practical restrictions on any programme that you choose. For example, it's important to remember *not* to do any relaxation exercises too soon after a meal or after lively physical exercise; you need time for your body to digest its food or to cool down before you begin your relaxation programme. By the same token, you shouldn't try any relaxation techniques after even moderate drinking since alcohol depresses the central nervous system and lessens your ability to control your mind and body.

Many of the relaxation techniques can be practised at any time, but it is probably better to observe a routine based on the following points:

- **Make it regular**   Put aside a regular slot of approximately 20 minutes each day for relaxation at a time that's convenient for you and/or when you feel at your best.

- **Get comfortable**   Choose a place with a comfortable environment, i.e. one that's not too cold or hot, too noisy or quiet, or too light or dark. Lie flat on your back on the floor if you can, or sit in on a hard chair with good back support. Loosen any articles of clothing that could constrict your breathing. Take your shoes off.

- **Be passive**   Although some relaxation techniques involve consciously regressing to a more relaxed state free from anxiety, don't try to force it. Let relaxation happen *to* you rather than try to *make* it happen.

Relaxation techniques

There are many ways of achieving a state of relaxation including *relaxation response exercises, deep muscle relaxation,* and *self-suggestion.* Examples of each of these techniques are described below. Try all of them and decide which one(s) you find the most enjoyable and the most convenient for you.

Relaxation response exercise

This exercise will introduce you to the relaxation response:

1. Choose a suitable place to relax in and assume a passive attitude.

2. Focus on your breathing. Try to make it as regular and uniform as possible. Maintain this rhythm throughout the whole exercise. Concentrate on any or all of the following images:

- Imagine the air that you're breathing is a cloud of vapour. With every breath you take in the cloud enters your expanding lungs and is exhaled along with unwanted tensions.

- Add colour to your cloud. Colour therapy is becoming accepted as part of stress relief and can add an extra dimension to feelings of release. You can choose any colour you want, but some are believed to have more positive associations than others. Yellow is associated with calm reflection. Green is believed to represent harmony, and blue coolness and tranquillity. Mix your colours.

- Visualize the expansion of your lungs as a balloon being inflated; as you exhale, the balloon deflates.

- As you inhale, silently say the word 'in' to yourself; as you exhale, say the word 'out'.

3. Relax by concentrating on your chosen image. If your thoughts start to wander, bring them back to focus on your word or image.

4. Deepen your relaxed state either by counting backwards slowly from ten to one, or by visualizing yourself walking down a long, sweeping spiral staircase. With each number counted or with each step descended, feel a deeper sense of peace and calm.

5. Return to a more alert state by slowly counting from one to five. On five, open your eyes. You should be feeling calm, relaxed and alert. Try to maintain this state for the rest of the day. It helps if you remember to breathe deeply and evenly.

Deep muscle relaxation

This technique involves isolating muscles in the body and tensing and relaxing them in a specific and fixed order from the head to the feet. It is best if you lie flat on your back on the floor, although it is possible to do it on a chair if you prefer.

The procedure is straightforward. Perform each of the individual muscle contraction drills twice before progressing on to the next. Hold each tensed position for five seconds. Feel the tension in your body slipping away. Don't rush it.

1. Tense the muscles in your forehead. Try to bring your eyebrows together at the bridge of your nose. Relax.

2. Close your eyes as tightly as you can. Flare your nostrils. Relax.

3. Draw your lips back in a grimace. Tense the muscles in your jawline. Relax.

4. Shrug your shoulders up towards your ears. Tense the muscles at the sides of your neck. Relax.

5. Bring your arms straight down to your sides and push them as hard as possible into your body. Relax.

6. Bend your elbows and tense your biceps. Relax.

7. Straighten your arms. Try to bend your elbows in the 'wrong' direction. Feel the muscles underneath your arms tighten. Relax.

8. Straighten your arms. Splay your fingers. Feel all of the muscles in your forearms. Relax.

9. Clench your fists as tightly as you can. Relax.

10. Concentrate on your back. Try to press it to the floor. Relax. **DO NOT** arch your back as this might cause or accentuate back trouble.

11. Pull your stomach muscles together while at the same time breathing out. Relax. Remember to keep all parts of your back firmly on the floor.

12. Clench your buttocks together as tightly as you can. Relax.

13. Tighten your thigh muscles. Try to keep your heels slightly off the floor. Relax.

14. Point your toes and feel your calf muscles tighten. Relax. Be careful, some people can occasionally experience cramps with this exercise.

15. Flex your ankles up towards your head as far as they can go. Relax.

16. Try to curl your toes underneath themselves. Relax.

Self-suggestion

In this exercise you repeat a word formula as a focused reminder to relax each part of your body. You need not say the words out loud; just repeat them to yourself in the sequence given below.

1. Lie on the floor or sit upright on a firm chair and assume a passive attitude.

2. Slowly repeat this formula to yourself:

- My right arm is heavy – My right arm is heavy
- My left arm is heavy – My left arm is heavy

- My arms are heavy and warm – My arms are heavy and warm
- My arms are heavy and warm; I can feel the warmth spreading to my hands
- My arms are heavy and warm; I can feel the warmth spreading to my hands
- My right leg is heavy – My right leg is heavy
- My left leg is heavy – My left leg is heavy
- My legs are heavy and warm – My legs are heavy and warm
- My legs are heavy and warm; I can feel the warmth spreading to my feet
- My legs are heavy and warm; I can feel the warmth spreading to my feet
- My breathing is steady and calm – My breathing is steady and calm
- My breathing is steady and calm; I feel calm and relaxed
- My breathing is steady and calm; I feel calm and relaxed
- I feel calm and relaxed
- I feel calm and relaxed
- I feel calm and relaxed

I sometimes use this formula lying in bed just before I go to sleep and find it helps, after I've finished, to imagine the weight of my worries slowly rising off my skin as a warm vapour.

Quick relaxation techniques

There will be times during the day when you will find yourself becoming tense and anxious. Often it happens for no apparent reason and when it does it may be impractical to lie down and perform a twenty-minute relaxation exercise. Nevertheless, you will need to have a way of eliciting a relaxed state of mind.

The following are examples of quick relaxation techniques:

- **Releasing body tension** Tense all the muscles in your whole body for as long as you can. Gradually relax your muscles and feel your anxiety and tension slipping away. Repeat three times.

- **Counting from ten to one** Even though something (or someone) has upset you, try to remain calm and indifferent. Take deep and even breaths, counting them backwards from ten to one. Feel your body become more relaxed.

- **Focusing on a spot** Relax your body. Choose a spot to focus on. Count slowly backwards from ten to one. On 'one' your eyes should be closed and you should be feeling relaxed.

- **Imagining air as a cloud** Focus on your breathing; let it become regular and even. Imagine the air around you as a cloud of cooling vapour that fills your lungs, bringing welcome relief. Feel the heat of your anger or anxiety flow out when you exhale.

- **Using worry beads or 'executive toys'** Try using worry beads as an aid to relaxation. The repeated action of feeling the beads (and possibly repeating a mantra – see page 98) can help in blocking out anxiety and stress. There are a number of commercial products that are designed to achieve the same effect. These are normally soft balls, or an equivalent, which can be squeezed and regain their shape when pressure is released. Choose what you want. I keep a pair of traditional Chinese iron spheres in my office that are used by placing them in the palm of the hand and moving them in a circular pattern with the fingers. They help me when I'm thinking negatively or beginning to feel stressed-out.

You may feel that even with all of these methods at your disposal you're never quite relaxed. It's especially difficult if your partner has died and you are now forced to live alone. You'll inevitably miss the joy of reaching out and being comforted. A partial support is to get a pet. Having a pet such as a dog around can be a great solace. When treated with affection, animals give almost unconditional love in return. It has been proven that the action of petting a dog or stroking a cat can bring about a great reduction in stress, anxiety and tension. You can talk to an animal without feeling self-conscious and, while it may not be a substitute for human contact, the companionship of a pet can bring happiness and relaxation.

Meditation techniques

For some people meditation is inevitably associated with mysticism and religion. This doesn't have to be the case. Meditation, whether in isolation or as part of a more spiritual approach to life, is a valuable tool for relaxation. However, what I will describe here is a technique applicable to someone who has recently been bereaved, without extensive reference to religious beliefs or spiritual convictions.

There are a number of other misconceptions about meditation that make people reluctant to try it. It's often believed that meditation is the process of shutting yourself off from reality by falling into a trance-like state and losing yourself in abstract thought; ultimately you forget where you are.

Many people, quite incorrectly, assume that there isn't much difference between meditation and self-hypnosis. In fact, the aim of meditation is to focus thought and keep the mind alert and attentive. Unlike the drowsiness of a trance or of hypnosis, the end result of meditation is increased awareness. Meditation can be divided into two different types:

- meditation associated with the five senses

- meditation intended to shut out unwanted thoughts

Meditation using the senses

On a surface level many of the following exercises might appear to have little obvious point. You will not gain any great or worthwhile knowledge from them, nor will you feel particularly enlightened spiritually. However, when you have finished you will have achieved something: a deeper level of calm and relaxation. Try all of the different types of sense meditation and stay with the one that suits you. Most of them can be done at any time; you do not need to go to a 'special' place. You can exercise in your office at lunchtime if you want, or at home if you haven't decided to return to or start work yet. Each exercise should last ten minutes.

The object of meditation using the senses is to extend a perception of the senses and, through this process, prevent the intrusion of unwanted thoughts. Such thoughts might include a desperate wish to be able to go back in time and 'right' all the 'wrongs' you did to your partner, family member or friend and

---

Sense of touch meditation

Choose an object that you think would be interesting to touch and feel. It can be *anything*, perhaps something from your desk or a natural object such as a leaf or stone.

1. Sit down and get comfortable.

2. Take the object in your hands and close your eyes.

3. *Slowly* start feeling it, using all of your fingers. What shape is it? Is it rough, smooth, crusty or scaly? Is it warm? Is it malleable? Explore its edges. Are they sharp or rounded?

4. Try to merge your thoughts with the object.

5. Relax.

---

unsay all the hurtful things you said. You might be overwhelmed by a sense of loneliness and loss. Negative thoughts of this nature *will* intrude from time to time, but you will find that you will be able to deal with them better if you try to eliminate them through meditation.

Sense of smell meditation

People appear to respond in a variety of ways when exposed to the same smell or scent. It is thought by many that exposure to aromas can have a beneficial effect on mood and lessen stress and anxiety. This premise has led to the establishment of the aromatherapy industry. Aromatherapy uses essential oils distilled from plants that can be vaporized through a diffuser specifically designed for the purpose and breathed in. These readily available oils can be used with meditation.

Find an oil with a scent that you like, or think you might find interesting to discover more about, as opposed to an oil that could have other beneficial properties. You don't have to restrict yourself to a scented oil. You can quite easily examine the smells of everyday objects, a lemon cut in half for instance, and still achieve the same goal of relaxation.

Choose a suitable place to explore the scent you've chosen. If you are using an oil, put a couple of drops on a diffuser and let the scent fill the room. Try to cut out interference from your other senses; draw the blinds or curtains, keep noise levels down to a minimum, wear loose clothes that aren't restrictive.

1. Gently close your eyes and concentrate on the scent. Is it strong, light, heavy or sweet? Is there a combination of smells that you think you can identify?

2. Try to merge your thoughts with the scent.

3. Relax.

Sense of sight meditation

Choose an object to look at. It may help if the object is something that you can unwrap or peel; you can examine a whole range of surfaces and compare them.

1. Get comfortable.

2. Take the object and *slowly* examine it minutely. If you want, you can use a magnifying glass.

3. Try to determine the nature of the object you've chosen. Is there a particular sheen to it? Is its surface pitted or smooth? Does its quality appear to change in the light? Have you noticed any differences on closer examination compared to a quick first glance?

4. Try to merge your thoughts with what you are seeing.

5. Relax.

Sense of hearing meditation

Most of the time we tend to shut out extraneous noise and try to focus on a very narrow range of sounds. The reason for this is quite straightforward. We want, for instance, to concentrate on what someone is saying in order not to miss anything. At other times we are so successful at subconsciously cutting off noise that we hardly notice just how much noise surrounds us. Sense of hearing meditation can make use of these two methods of listening.

To extend your conscious perception of hearing you can go to a place where you will hear a range of pleasant sounds. You could choose a local park and sit on a bench. Close your eyes and try to identify all of the sounds that you hear. You may be surprised.

Alternatively, you choose your favourite music and concentrate on *listening* to it rather than playing it as background music. Clearly, softer and more melodic music will be more conducive to relaxation than uptempo pieces, although dramatic music *can* trigger deeper feelings of relaxation.

Another way of extending your perception of your sense of hearing is to eliminate all other sounds and concentrate on a new sound that you have never heard before:

1. Find a comfortable place to sit or lie down.

2. Take some grains of dry rice or some paper clips and make a loose fist. Shake the rice grains, paper clips, or anything else that you think would make an interesting sound, and listen.

3. What different sounds can you produce if you vary the way in which you rattle what you have in your hand? Can you produce a range of sounds? Do the sounds remind you of anything? Tighten your fist and grind the items into the palm of your hand. What difference is there in the quality of the sound?

4. Try to merge your thoughts with the sounds.

5. Relax.

Sense of taste meditation

You can easily do the following exercise in your office at lunchtime or at home. Select a range of foods with different flavours and textures. You might want to make this a comparative study by taking, for example, varieties of the same fruit and trying to establish the difference between them.

1. Close the door to your room or office and get comfortable.

2. Choose a portion of food at random.

3. Bite into it *slowly* and try to establish what combination of tastes comprise the food's flavour. Is it spicy, bitter, sour or sweet? Does it leave an aftertaste? Is there a grainy quality to the food that is part of the flavour?

4. Try to merge your thoughts with the tastes.

5. Relax.

Meditation to shut out unwanted thoughts

Sometimes, despite all efforts to develop a framework of positive thoughts about your future without your loved one, it happens that you are caught unaware by events. A chance remark or even the way someone on the street carries themselves can release a torrent of memories. It's also easy to torment yourself by recalling incidents that you deeply regret. However much you are told: 'It's in the past. Let it *go* . . .', it's not unusual to find yourself becoming lost in an agony of grief and despair.

There is a whole range of meditation techniques that are intended to help the meditator shut out thought in order to be more able to come to an understanding of their own nature and place in the universe. This is perhaps what most people (often dismissively) perceive to be the purpose of meditation. But there is no need to regard the following techniques as anything other than another series of relaxation methods. They are only suggested here as a means of countering the anxieties and stresses of bereavement. Yet again, each exercise should last about ten minutes.

Among the shutting-out meditation techniques that you can use are visualization, focusing, sound, and breathing. If you prefer, there is a less restrictive, 'methodless', style of meditation that you might find more easy to take up.

Visualization exercises

When unwanted thoughts or feelings of regret come tumbling into your mind you can use a range of images to block them out. They can be of anything that you want but, of course, positive, happy images are best. It is possible to visualize yourself regaining control of the positive qualities of self-worth, which, in your darker moments, you despair of ever regaining. Visualize yourself being in good spirits, chatting again with friends or going on your favourite walk – maybe alone – and enjoying it.

If these don't help, then visualize yourself building a brick wall between you and the thoughts that you don't want; if the thoughts seem to be trying to intrude, build your wall quicker, thicker and higher.

Focusing exercise

If you find it too exhausting to create images, you might want to focus your thoughts on a real object and, by doing so, release your tension. A common point of focus in meditation is a candle's flame.

Look into the flame and see how it flickers and changes shape. If negative thoughts try to break into your concentration, increase your focus on the flame.

You might find it difficult to keep your eyes fixed on the flame without starting to blink repeatedly, or your eyes beginning to water. This isn't unusual. If this happens, simply close your eyes every few seconds and visualize the flame in your mind's eye before you open them again.

Relax after ten minutes.

Sound

Perhaps the most recognized, and scoffed at, meditative form is one where thoughts are blocked with gently spoken chants. These are more commonly known as *mantras*. It is believed that the resonance of the sounds in mantras has a special quality that helps in transcending the constraints of 'normal' experience and reaching a higher level of understanding.

Chanting is a tradition of both Eastern and Western religions. Some branches of the Orthodox Church, for example, make use of the Jesus prayer: 'Lord Jesus Christ, Son of God, Have Mercy on Me', while the Greek Orthodox, Roman Catholic and Anglican Churches all use the invocation: 'Kyrie Eleison' (Lord Have Mercy). Followers of an Eastern meditative tradition use, among others, the mantras: 'Om Mani Padme Hum' (Hail to the Jewel in the Lotus), and the healing mantra of Padmasambhava, the founder of Tibetan Buddhism, 'Om Ah Vajra Guru Padma Siddhi Hum'.

Mantras and chants are not ends in themselves, but just a way of using sound to bring about an altered state of consciousness and, because of the quality of their sounds, drive away thought. Their meaning is often secondary, and indeed, any word or phrase repeated often enough will appear to lose its associated meaning and become nonsensical. However, it probably helps to choose a chant or mantra that has some meaning for you as well as for its sound quality.

Posture is important in reciting mantras, as good posture allows you to breathe more easily. Sit with your legs crossed and your back straight. It helps if you place your hands palms down on your knees. You can keep your eyes open or closed as you wish. Recite your mantra slowly and quietly, paying attention to breath control and the quality of the sounds you produce. Keep reciting the mantra for ten minutes. Relax silently in the same position for two or three minutes after you have finished chanting.

Breathing exercise

One of the symptoms of anxiety and stress is shallowness and shortness of breath. Breathing exercises are one way of checking these symptoms and, at the same time, shutting out the unwanted thoughts that can be the cause of the initial anxiety.

Find a comfortable place to relax in and consciously turn your attention to your breathing.

1. Try to be conscious of your breathing just as a sensation. Feel the changing nature of the air as you breathe it in and out. Notice how it becomes warmer as you exhale.

2. Draw your breath down deep into you, consciously using the diaphragm to expand your lungs, and relax.

3. Choose a point of breathing to focus on. The obvious choice is the sensitive area of the nostrils where sensation is at its greatest. You could also choose to focus on the abdomen, which might give you a greater feeling of whole body control.

4. Count the breaths that you take and feel your anxiety flowing out with each breath that you exhale.

Methodless meditation

Meditation does not necessarily have to fit one of the patterns outlined above. Meditation can be viewed as *anything* that elicits a relaxation response. Movement can be considered as meditation. If you find dancing or gymnastics, or even fishing, relaxing to the degree that you lose yourself in concentration, then you could justifiably call this meditation. Similarly, painting, writing or singing could be classified as meditation.

It doesn't matter *what* you do to achieve a relaxed state of mind. With methodless meditation it's quite simply a case of the end justifying the means.

six

Relationship skills for those who have lost a partner

Perhaps one of the last things on the mind of someone whose partner has died recently is the forming of new relationships with others. When a partner dies so does 'we'. Becoming 'I' again is an intensely harrowing process. At first, the grief of separation is so overwhelming that one has few thoughts – if any – of moving on (let alone of considering the huge step of new partnerships or re-marriage). However, things change. Initially, these changes are small. It's quite likely that at a relatively early stage you'll reassess the range of friendships you shared with your loved one. There will be people that you were acquainted with through your partner who you'll naturally grow apart from and drop over time. You might even want to pick up friendships from before.

It's difficult to make generalizations about the forming of new relationships after bereavement because different people have different needs and perceptions. For example, while some older widows or widowers eventually move on to other fulfilling relationships, others don't seem able to. Perhaps those who have been bereaved in later middle age or old age are less inclined to want to meet new people, let alone consider a more permanent alliance. However, there are those who do reach the stage of wanting to meet new people. After all, few of us can live a solitary life. Sometimes people re-marry.

It's very important to realize that relationships *aren't* just for the young. We *all* need the satisfaction of a loving group of people to support us and, possibly, the support of one special person. But the building of successful friendships with others is something that can require a great deal of work. It's especially hard for someone who has been bereaved; loneliness is one of their biggest problems. The purpose of this chapter is to present some ideas about friendship to think about, and to give practical hints on meeting new people.

Perhaps a good point of focus for understanding how to form new relationships after the devastation of bereavement is to consider what came before. You will have had good and bad relationships with a wide range of people before the death of your loved one. These can reveal what attitudes you brought to a successful relationship and how others didn't work out.

Complete the following task:

1. Think of three to five people with whom you've shared satisfying and fulfilling relationships. Write down all the reasons why you believe the relationships were successful. What behaviour or attitudes did you have that helped to make them fulfilling?

2. List three to five people with whom you've had poor relationships. Write down the reasons why you think these relationships didn't work out. What attitudes or behaviour did you have that helped to make them fail?

3. With the above reasons in mind, decide which types of behaviour and attitudes you should alter or suppress if you want to keep your present (and future) relationships healthy and positive.

Meeting new people

Making contact with new people is difficult even at the best of times. Most people are constantly battling with a negative internal monologue that prevents them from initiating a conversation: 'She wouldn't want to talk to *me* . . .'; 'I'm useless at meeting new people . . .'; 'Let's face it, I'm too *old*, too *fat* and too *stupid* to attract anyone decent . . .' As if this wasn't enough, we also have to contend with an archaic and restrictive social code that hinders the development of friendly and familiar relations between people. Until recently it wasn't considered appropriate for someone to initiate a conversation with anyone they'd not previously been introduced to, with the result that many people still feel that it's not 'right', or that it would be excessively forward, to introduce themselves. Similarly, people are uncomfortable with the idea of approaching a stranger in public unless they are asking for directions or something else equally innocuous.

And then for everyone who meets a new person there is the issue of prejudgement. This is the largely unconscious practice of making critical interpretations of someone's personality when we meet them for the first time. Our impressions depend on the influences of our previous experiences, and the values and assumptions that are part of our personality. These prejudgements are usually made on the basis of 'approval' or 'disapproval', resulting in a black-and-white evaluation of whether a person is, for example, warm-hearted or ice-cold, friendly or aloof, intelligent or stupid. From these intuitive judgements we decide on the relative 'goodness' or 'badness' of the person in front of us.

Research into prejudgement suggests that these first impressions tend to stick, even if they are later proved false. In general, we only make minor revisions to our initial perception of someone's personality even after months of occasional meetings with the other person.

There are, almost naturally, extra difficulties for the newly bereaved when they meet people. They have to decide whether to tell the person that their partner died. This is a personal decision governed by circumstances and character. However, if you *do* tell someone, you trigger a whole set of assumptions in the mind of the hearer, who interprets your status and outlook from *their* perspective and *their* set of values and experiences.

It's likely that you'll be given the label 'widow/er' (or be thought of as such if you were not married to your partner) in the same way that a person is labelled a 'bachelor' or 'spinster'. Think about these last two words. They have fairly simple, central meanings. A bachelor is 'an unmarried man' and a spinster is 'an unmarried woman'. But they also carry a set of implied meanings that colour these central meanings. For example, 'bachelor' might have associated meanings of being carefree, debonair and happy, while in contrast 'spinster' is a highly loaded and derogatory term. It seems to have a more negative evaluative and emotional significance than 'bachelor'. For many people it would convey: old, sad, 'on the shelf', isolated and lonely.

It's difficult to know with any certainty the implied meanings of 'widow' and 'widower'. Perhaps there's a slight mirroring of the imbalance between 'bachelor' and 'spinster'. It's probably the case that both words in isolation indicate: old, sad and lonely, but there may be a sense that 'widower' carries an extra level of commiseration which could result from the fact that there are considerably more widows than widowers, and a perception that widowers are perhaps less capable of looking after themselves domestically.

Certainly, there's a difference in implied meanings between the labels 'widow/er' and the label 'single person'. On a conceptual level they can denote the same thing: a person who isn't married. For instance, if you were at a social gathering and were asked the question: 'Are you married or with someone?', you could reply: 'I'm single' or 'I'm on my own' and be received neutrally. Yet if you replied: 'I'm a widow/er' or 'I had a long-term partner, but she/he died' this would elicit a set of speculative assumptions in the mind of the listener. They could reasonably infer that you are very sad, feeling lost and brimming with grief. As a result, they might not continue a normal lighthearted 'party' conversation, thinking it inappropriate.

They might also perceive you to be emotionally distant and untouchable, which they wouldn't presume in the case of a person who's simply 'single'. They might reason that a single person could be single through choice, whereas there isn't a choice in being separated by death from a partner who will always be a part of you emotionally, thus making you indifferent to meeting new people. This may explain the marked degree of hesitancy in people who know you as a 'widow/er' even if all the evidence proves you are no longer excessively sad or lost and you have started to manage your grief.

These factors make it extremely difficult to judge if or when to tell someone what has happened. As a rule, it is probably better *not* to volunteer any information until it seems natural or necessary to you. Remember that you aren't obliged to tell anyone your circumstances. Do it only if it feels right. If you aren't comfortable answering people's direct questions about your status you don't have to give a direct answer.

Whatever the case, it's important to put the fear of meeting new people into proportion. If you have a positive sense of self-worth then it is unlikely that you will feel threatened at the thought of meeting people. However, someone who has been bereaved is likely to feel vulnerable, believing that their already shaky plans for the future might be further undermined by social rejection. As a result they tend to withdraw and become defensive; attitudes that do not help in building positive relationships. It is essential to reframe these attitudes if you are to form successful and meaningful relationships.

Coping strategies

- **Adjust your approach** When people think about approaching someone that they are attracted to it's quite usual for them to have an idea in their heads of how the other person will perceive them. Often this is negatively framed. At a social gathering these thoughts might be manifested as: 'Ah, he's nice, but he won't really see anything in me . . .'; or, in the context of a competitive work situation, the thoughts might be: 'She'll probably think I want something from her . . .' Both of these prejudgements, and others of this type, tend to frame the meeting as a test. It's a test that the person has already convinced themselves they're going to fail. It's imperative that this form of approach is dropped. Meeting someone should not be viewed as a test to see if you're attractive enough to sleep with, whether you're going to end up friends with that person, or if indeed they're going to like you. Wanting to meet someone is *only* an offer to share some time and nothing more.

- **Reassess your negative internal monologue** Think about the following situation. You are in a dentist's waiting room and you start a conversation with someone you're attracted to. They listen to what you say for a few moments and make a few casual responses before the conversation dies. What would your inner voice be saying to you at that stage? It might be saying that you were 'ridiculous' to even think about starting a conversation or that you are always 'foolish' in public. This kind of habitual negative labelling prevents you from wanting to carry on just talking to people. Instead you should try and avoid such judgemental labels. You're not 'foolish' or 'ridiculous' in wanting to talk to someone, you're just making a casual everyday attempt to engage someone else in conversation. Use thought-stopping whenever you find your internal monologue trying to get the upper hand. If you're objective about situations you find yourself in, you'll be better able to cope.

- **Reframe rejection** If you offer to share some time with someone that you're attracted to you, you *may* find that your offer will be rejected – in much the same way that the attempt to make conversation was rejected in the 'waiting room' example above. You can react to this rejection by listening to your negative internal monologue which tells you that the other person thinks you are 'incompetent' or 'stupid'. You might conclude that they think you are so unattractive that they don't want to get to know you better. However, you don't actually know *why* they don't want to go to the movies or chat over a coffee. You are interpreting their reaction to your offer in the most negative way possible. Try to put yourself in their position. There may be a whole host of reasons why you wouldn't want to talk over a coffee or spend an evening at the multiplex with a relative stranger. You may just have had a coffee break, you could have seen the movie already, or you might have some letters that you want to write that can't wait. Quite simply, you might be in the mood to have some time alone to yourself that evening. So, why imagine that someone else has other, less ordinary, reasons?

Getting acquainted

The only way to get to acquainted with someone is to start a conversation. You can more or less safely assume that the person you want to talk to has fears of being embarrassed or rejected, just as you do, but really *does* want to meet people, so you shouldn't get worried about breaking the ice.

Obviously, when we meet people a lot of information is communicated, but much of it is revealed through our body language as well as through the words we speak. Body language can signal levels of attentiveness in terms of interest or disinterest, willingness to listen, indifference or fascination, all of which have an effect on the outcome of the conversation. It's largely unconscious, but it's a set of behaviours that you can learn in order to make getting acquainted an easier and less stressful experience. These behaviours fall into the categories of eye contact, facial expression and body posture.

- **Eye contact**   A primary indicator of attentiveness is whether or not you make frequent eye contact with the person you're talking and listening to. When you look down or away it shows that you're nervous or that your mind is elsewhere. Equally, making eye contact can be stressful. If you stare at the other person or if your expression is blank, you'll make them feel uncomfortable. If you are uneasy or embarrassed about looking into someone's eyes then look at their nose, ear or mouth. They won't be able to tell that you're not looking in their eyes.

- **Facial expression**   Facial expressions tell the person you're talking to that you're interested in what they have to say. Smiles, nods, frowns and raised eyebrows are all part of a normal conversation. However, the rule is not too much and not too little. Smile and nod too much and you'll end up looking (and, in fact, being) insincere. Smile, nod and raise your eyebrows infrequently and you'll seem cold, distant and unemotional. Let your emotions show, but be *genuine*.

- **Body posture**   The key to body posture in conversation is being relaxed. By not crossing your arms and legs and by leaning slightly forward, you are indicating you're open and willing to talk. When you cross your arms you're putting across a defensive mental attitude, so avoid it if you can. If you want to emphasize a point you can do this by occasional arm and hand movements. Of course, you don't want to encroach on anyone's personal space so just keep a distance that seems comfortable.

Of course, a good conversation is more than body language or even just words. It's also about attitudes. It's when the speakers show respect for each other, empathize with each other and are genuine in their intentions towards each other.

Respect in a conversation is shown by attending to what the other person has to say. This means that you are willing to give up your time to hear what they have to say rather than just saying what *you* want to say. Respect is also shown by asking questions. It shows that you value what the other person has to say and tells them that you're *actively* listening rather than *passively* shutting up before it's 'your turn' to speak again. Empathy is marked by a sharing and exchange of experiences which shows that you can identify with what the speaker is saying; you are indicating that you understand how they view the world. Finally, if you are genuine – that is, being sincere, natural and yourself and not acting a part – it shows the person you're talking to that you can be trusted. When they see this they're more likely to respond positively to you, and so your conversation is more likely to be successful.

However, you may not feel as though you want to try and empathize with the person in front of you. Surely, *they* should be trying to empathize with you? After all, it's *you* who's had the misery and heartache. This attitude, and others like it, is very understandable. Unfortunately, it will hinder, rather than help, in the forming of satisfying and healthy relationships. It's important to see things from the other person's point of view. They may not have any experience or understanding of your circumstances. It would be unfair of you to impose your values on them. If you are always trying to push the conversation your way, then it's likely to fail.

Similarly, if you are unwilling to disclose information about yourself it's likely that your conversation will be short-lived. This doesn't mean that you immediately reveal your most intimate details to the relative stranger in front of you, such as the fact that you have recently suffered a bereavement, but if you don't tell them anything about yourself it's unlikely that their interest will be sustained.

This process of self-disclosure exists on three levels. The first of these is simply informational and could include details such as your name, job and job history, where you last went on holiday, or maybe a funny thing that happened to you recently. The second is slightly more intimate and includes disclosing information about your beliefs, values, needs and wants. Typically, these might include details of a value system that you are strongly committed to, the politics you hold or your hopes for the future. It might also involve details of your past which you could tell as a story against yourself. This is all very risky because you have to be willing to reveal information that might convince the other person you're *not* someone they want to spend more time with. However, it's worth noting that it's better not to hold back too much in this second level because by being unnecessarily secretive you're stifling any meaningful emotional closeness.

The final level is almost certainly the most stressful since it involves disclosing how you feel about the person you're talking to. Inevitably, this not only involves telling them how much you might like them, but also all those little things that you have difficulty accepting, such as how the other person responds to what you have to say. In addition, you could tell them what you hope will come out of your being together. As with all of these levels of self-disclosure, there is no set rule as to when you should go from one to the other. Just trust your judgement and disclose information when it feels right.

Keeping a relationship going

Of all the many people you'll meet after your loved one has died there may be one or two that you'll want to keep as friends. You might have interests and values in common, share the same set of friends and find that you can talk easily together. More importantly, they might support you as a friend when you're in trouble, going beyond the levels of commiseration of most people, who view you simply as a widow/er or bereaved parent. You might feel that they are people on whom you can depend.

These are some of the essential qualities that are necessary in any relationship that is to be maintained. Of course, it's possible to ruin the development of any healthy relationship by trying to manipulate the other person into doing things for you because they feel sympathy towards you. Similarly, you could easily end a relationship by telling lies to this person, talking behind their back, or being unreliable and then blaming it on your bereavement. Being secretive is another fast route to ending any meaningful friendship.

Inevitably, you will find that at times you disagree with what the other person has to say and what they do, but the key to keeping a relationship going is to accept that the other person has different ideas from yours and not try to change them. If there *are* differences that you feel need addressing, then try to reach an agreement through compromise by talking calmly to the person. If you fail then this is not something that necessarily reflects on either of you. Sometimes things just don't work out. Remember that it's possible, however, to grow apart and still remain on friendly terms. By the same token, just because things don't work out, it doesn't mean that the whole experience of knowing someone was worthless.

Paratactic distortion

Unfortunately, things don't always go so smoothly for someone who's been bereaved. This applies to meeting new people as much as anything else. Fears and feelings of lack of self-worth can become amplified and the outcome is that some people try to overcompensate. The anxiety and panic brought on by death tempts people to make hasty or unwise decisions. Some feel lonely and incomplete without their loved one and, in a confused attempt to replace them, rush headlong into a new and unsuitable relationship or try to pick up the pieces of an old one.

It isn't unusual for someone whose partner died not long ago to ascribe characteristics to new people they meet which are not consistent with objective reality. A voice, a hairstyle or even a gesture can lead them to associate the qualities and values of their loved one with the person in front of them.

This phenomenon is known to psychologists as *paratactic distortion*, but is more commonly referred to as 'being on the rebound'. It can lead to embarrassing confusion, misunderstanding and deep hurt. It is important to recognize the existence of the possibility that you might unconsciously superimpose a set of beliefs and assumptions on someone you meet, or someone you used to know, and guard against it. Whenever you feel strongly attracted to someone you meet, especially in the first few months after your loved one has died, ask yourself these questions:

1. Does this person *really* have the same values my partner had? Do they react to the same situations in the same way?

2. What does this person *really* want and feel? Do I *know* what they want and feel or am I *assuming* that I know?

If you don't know the answers to these questions, find out. But be warned. If you *do* discover that you've been seeing things that aren't there, this does not necessarily mean that you will stop seeing them. Studies conclude that even after finding out that someone doesn't have the values you associate with a past partner, the feelings you hold and attitudes you have towards the person in the present are not easily dislodged. For instance, you might have evidence that the current person in your life holds a set of beliefs that you fundamentally disagree with, but because of the way they laugh or smile – just like your loved one used to – you *know* that 'deep down' they have qualities that you admire and respect, and that with time this person will come to realize that you're made for each other.

Of course, they almost never do, but the tantalizing hope is always there, and so confusion, embarrassment and potential humiliation are very possible outcomes when these expectations are not realized. To avoid this, try to clear up any potential misperceptions as soon as you can. One way is to adopt the following approach: by the end of the first meeting with the new person:

- tell them that you want to know them better (if you do), or explain how you feel about them

- state what happened during the meeting according to your point of view

- state what you hope and expect from the other person

- allow the other person to correct or object to any false impressions you might have

Initially you might find this kind of approach threatening because you may be reluctant to reveal your feelings when you are feeling so vulnerable; there is a lot of potential here for being knocked back or rejected by the other person. However, finding out exactly how someone else is feeling and thinking is preferable to labouring under a set of assumptions that prove false in the long run.

seven

Decision-making skills

Delaying decisions

It may seem an odd idea to start a chapter on decision-making skills by saying 'don't make any decisions', but probably the best advice for anyone who has just suffered a bereavement is: don't make *any* major decisions that will bring about great changes to your life, such as changing job, moving house or trying to rebuild your life in a new town – at least not just yet. If you can, wait. The reason is *not* so that you don't have to make them (you will), but to allow yourself time to work through the worst of your grief and *then* decide what you have to do. This waiting period may take a year. For some people it's a little bit less and for others a little more. It depends on your age, personality, previous experiences and the circumstances surrounding the death.

Certainly, some people may feel they don't have the luxury of a year. *If their partner has died*, they might have to confront the reality of stark economic hardship brought on by the death and take on an extra job to make ends meet, or sell their home and move into a smaller one. But if you don't *have* to move or to take new employment, then don't do it just for the sake of it or because you feel you have to do *something*. It's likely that you'll regret a quick decision. Allow the momentum of life to carry you through. Although you may not believe this, it will.

The reason for delaying decisions is that the death of a spouse or child is generally considered to be the most stressful single event that anyone can face, and the death of a brother, sister, uncle, aunt or grandparent may be only marginally less so, depending on how closely-knit your family is. The emotional response accompanying such a bereavement is usually hopelessness and helplessness and, under this kind of pressure, it's almost impossible to make clear and balanced choices. Your confidence and self-worth will be seriously undermined and it's likely that you'll have found yourself thinking: 'I don't know what to do . . .' or 'I'll never be able to cope . . .' You might even think about giving up completely, since for you life has become meaningless. Quite simply, most people who have been newly bereaved are almost certainly not in the right frame of mind to make good, careful decisions regarding life choices. They can easily allow themselves to listen to others and be swayed into taking decisions against their better judgement because their defences are down.

And, if you think about it, making unnecessary, hasty decisions just piles on extra pressure and increases self-destructive frustration and anxiety at a time when you have more than enough troubles. In my own case, I'd had excessive stress and worry leading up to Shirin's death. In the two months before she died I completed a contract in China, sat four examinations in London, thought seriously about buying a house, accepted a position in Brunei (a part of the world I'd never visited before), and grew more worried and helpless as Shirin's health slowly worsened just a few weeks after we'd arrived. The fact that none of the doctors knew what was wrong with her merely added to my levels of stress.

Yet, after her funeral back in Britain, rather than allow myself to go with life's flow, my initial reaction was to throw away everything that I'd worked for, give up my new job and try to start afresh; I could not, and did not, believe I would cope with a new job in a strange place without Shirin. However, the sad truth is that I was able to cope – after a fashion. It wasn't easy and I'd certainly never have wished it, but I *was* able to carry on. It was only after some eight or nine months that I found that I was ready to think a little more clearly about the future.

I cannot emphasize too much how important it is to allow yourself time to grieve, not to rush, and to *wait* until your emotions are more stable before taking decisions that may have an enormous effect on your future.

Initial decisions . . . saying 'no'

However, whatever your personality or circumstances, there are *some* choices that you'll have to make straight away. Will your loved one be buried or cremated? Do you want flowers at the funeral? What will you do with your loved one's clothes and other belongings? Will you accept the offer of a neighbour to sleep over at their place for a few nights?

These decisions are relatively minor compared to the 'life' choices you'll make which will affect your future. But they are *your* decisions. So don't allow anyone to pressurize you into something you don't want by saying things like: 'Oh! just get *rid* of all these things! You don't want them bringing back any bad memories for you'. or 'You *have to* have a big funeral with wreaths and hearses for all the family. You must to do it properly. You don't want anyone to think you didn't love or respect them, do you!'

Remember that you can listen to what others around you have to say, but you do not have to passively accept their advice. Be assertive. Being assertive is not the same as being aggressive. It doesn't involve raised voices, threats, arguments, accusations or demands. It is when you state what *you* want calmly, openly, honestly and politely.

The value in being assertive, especially at this time when you're likely to be feeling vulnerable and suggestible, is that you can avoid possible alienation of family and friends, and also frustration at your passivity in not taking responsibility for your choices. It helps if you can try and convey your message in a series of 'I' statements. 'I' statements show the person you're talking to that you are expressing your own feelings about something and not attacking them for holding a different opinion. Using 'I' statements isn't a case of you selfishly trying to take centre stage, it's being specific in what you want without being judgemental about what the other person is saying. Remember that most people are trying their best to help in what are also difficult circumstances for them; they aren't deliberately trying to be offensive.

By way of illustration, look at the difference in the following responses that could be made by a bereaved woman to a well-intentioned suggestion by a friend to clear out her husband's possessions soon after he has died:

1. 'You can't seriously expect me to just throw his things out as if he didn't exist! What a *dreadful* thing to suggest! You make me so *angry* when you say things like that! It's so hurtful! You don't understand at all!'

2. 'Yes, yes . . . you're right, I suppose . . . I mean . . . Well . . . all right. Just throw them out. Whatever you think's best.'

3. 'I know you think it would be a good idea to clear out these things, but they mean a lot to me. I feel very upset at the thought of throwing them out. I want to wait until I've thought carefully about what to do with them.'

The first of these possible responses is loaded with emotion and indicates blindness to the nature of her friend's suggestion. It shows someone lashing out in anger, intent on putting the other person down. It's likely that such a response will draw a similar level of anger from her friend or simply a refusal to help any more.

The second is hardly better because the bereaved woman has responded in a way that subordinates her wishes to those of her friend. Her thoughts and feelings are masked behind vague hints and rambling comments in a hope that her misgivings will be picked up. If she's lucky they will be, but it's quite possible that they won't. In such a situation, it's likely that in the weeks, months and years to come the bereaved woman will regret having passively accepted what her friend has suggested and, more often than not, blame her friend for it. But it's not her friend's fault. By accepting what her friend has suggested in this way the bereaved woman is giving her friend permission to take responsibility for the decision. And the chief responsibility for decisions of this type belongs to the bereaved.

A better and more constructive approach would be to react assertively in the 'I' statement style of the third response. It has four elements. First, the bereaved woman acknowledges what her friend has said (she could have asked for clarification if necessary) and, secondly, gives her own perspective on throwing the belongings away. Then, she presents her feelings non-threateningly and non-judgmentally. Finally, she gives a clear message of what she wants. In this case she decides to wait until she has thought about what she really wants to do, rather than make a snap decision. In this way she avoids bottling up frustrations and lowers the risk of confrontation. More importantly, she is able to take control and find a solution *she* wants *when* she wants.

At times like this use the following guidelines to assert what you want:

- be firm and consistent in what you say

- listen to the other person so that you can be sure of their feelings, opinions and wishes

- be honest in your reasons for refusing to agree to what the other person suggests

- don't put the other person down by accusing them of 'always making trouble' or 'trying to get their own way', as this will only lead to arguments and confrontation

- keep control of your emotions

So if you want to have a few hours by yourself in the home that you shared with your partner or family member, refuse the offer of a place to stay. If you don't want an expensive funeral, then say so. But if you do want to take up any of the generous offers or the suggestions that people will make, then accept them. But be assertive – not only in these instances, but in all of your subsequent decisions.

The decision-making process

After a suitable length of time, during which you've managed to gather yourself together and work through the greatest intensity of your grief, you should start the process of decision-making concerning life choices. Simply put, a decision of this type is a resolution made at a particular moment in time after the rational consideration of all reasonable options. The intended outcome of a decision is to achieve the greatest possible benefit for the person making the decision. This process has several stages, including: deciding the nature and context of the decision, gathering relevant facts, analysing these facts, and finally making a decision.

The decision-making process entails order, direction and discipline in your life, but after the death of your loved one you will probably feel frustrated and powerless. You will probably believe that you have little control of your future. This is an entirely understandable reaction. Why make plans if the person closest to you can be taken away from you without warning? What's the point? What control *do* you have over your life?

Reviewing your circumstances

It's important to find answers to these questions before you start gathering data to make your decision, since this will help in rebuilding your self-confidence and removing self-imposed barriers on decision-making. This can be achieved by reviewing your personal circumstances, which will not only make you face up to reality, but also allow you to see what the *actual* restrictions on your life and your ability to make decisions are. There is a vast range of things that you can change for the better (if you really want to) because in fact there are very few things that we are unable to change about ourselves. By realizing this you'll begin to take control of your life again rather than perhaps passively handing that responsibility over to external forces such as fate, destiny or luck.

One of the most effective methods of review is to look at all of the things that you *could* change *if* you wanted to, including your internal attitudes, health, outward behaviour, as well as the circumstances that surround you. First, take a piece of A4 paper and draw a chart with two columns like the one on the next page. Head the left-hand column 'Things I cannot change' and the right-hand column 'Things I can change'. A few examples have been done for you.

After you've finished, look at the lists you've made and think again. Do you see that you have far more control over yourself and your environment than you at first imagined? Are you sure that there aren't more items in the 'cannot change' column that could be moved to the 'can change' column? There may be a few that you can transfer, but *some* of the items in the 'cannot change' list are fixed. You cannot, for example, change the fact that your loved one is dead. Accept this and grieve, but don't torment yourself with worry and feelings of helplessness. Likewise, you won't be able to change your height, but you will be able to make other beneficial changes to your body that will result in better health and consequently a better quality of life, which is, ultimately, the main purpose of taking control of your life after the death of your loved one.

Things I **CANNOT** change	Things I **CAN** change
1. *The death of my loved one.*	**1.** *Financial situation.*
2. *Age.*	**2.** *Loss of self-worth.*
3. *Height.*	**3.** *Place and type of work.*
4.	**4.**
5.	**5.**
6.	**6.**
7.	**7.**
8.	**8.**
9.	**9.**
10.	**10.**
etc.	**etc.**

Defining the context of a decision

The first practical steps in the decision-making process are to acknowledge that a problem exists and then to define the context of any decision you will take. This is relatively easy and obvious in the case of something material like financial troubles. You might, for instance, have some difficulty in making mortgage payments on the property you shared with your partner, so you know that there is a problem caused by a lack of ready capital. Other difficulties, though, can be more elusive. You might conclude that you are unhappy, depressed, or just dissatisfied with life, and you're not too sure of a root cause other than an obvious sense of loss owing to your bereavement.

However, it's not so much the *causes* of the problem that are important in defining the context of a decision as the *effects* that will result if the problem you've identified is left unchecked. To say, for instance, that you have difficulty in making mortgage payments because you have no money, or that you are depressed because your loved one has died, isn't the whole story. Understanding the depth of a problem means being able to recognize the potential consequences and possible damage it can bring to your life. To do this you should try and project into the future and judge what could be the worst that could possibly happen if this problem was left to develop. In the case of not having enough money to keep up mortgage payments, the most likely worst outcome is that the house or flat will be repossessed.

Having determined the worst that can possibly happen, you should accept it as potentially real. You should be ready to reconcile yourself to it happening *despite* your efforts. By accepting the worst you'll be more able to see how to improve on it. In effect you are making a contract with yourself. You are agreeing to attempt to sort out your problems, knowing the extent of possible real outcomes. If the house *does* get repossessed, then you have failed after trying your best, which is entirely different to dithering about because you don't know the full scope of your problem, or (much worse) passively accepting your 'fate'.

Gathering facts

By accepting the worst-case scenario you should find that much of your anxiety disappears. You'll now be in a position to gather facts and information to help you in making your decision. To do this you need to collect a wide range of data, because if the decision isn't based on as much information as possible it's almost certainly going to be unreliable. Concentrate on gathering facts in an efficient and orderly fashion. (Don't attempt to interpret or evaluate any of these facts or pieces of information at this stage. That comes later.) There are three principal sources of facts:

- published material in books, newspapers, magazines and leaflets

- professionals who specialize in the information you're seeking

- friends or acquaintances who have some experience in the area

Use your local library. Talk to as many people as you can and don't be afraid to seek out people who have professional expertise. There are agencies you can turn to that provide free legal advice in most countries and states. Don't restrict yourself by ruling out some sources just because you're a little embarrassed or because they seem to be a little outlandish or unrealistic – they may not turn out to be. Don't be tempted to ignore some facts just because they might seem to be a little inconvenient.

Read all the information you can get your hands on, and listen to as many people as possible. Obviously, you will need to make notes. The basic equipment for note-taking is: pens, coloured pens, marker pens, A4 paper, files, notebooks, pencils, a hole punch, paper clips, staples and a stapler and, perhaps, a clipboard to lean on. None of this has to be expensive. Go for functionality rather than price. You need only buy a small pack of felt pens and maybe one or two marker pens. Lever-arch files are probably best because you can rearrange your notes as you want them and also put photocopies of articles or newspaper clippings in appropriate places. You may, of course, find plastic wallets or recycled paper wallet files more convenient.

As with all of the suggestions made here, what you use to make your notes is largely a matter of personal choice and habit. It's more important to pay attention to the kind of notes you make rather than the tools you use to make them. Notes are important for three reasons:

1. You can make a record of the *main ideas* of all the people you talk to and of all the information in the texts you read.

2. You have a means of absorbing information to make it become part of your knowledge.

3. You have your notes as an aid to memory.

You'll need to decide what form the notes will take, but what form should you choose? Again it's a question of what you feel comfortable with, but basically, you can record your information in a series of linear notes, or you can put the information in the form of branching notes, otherwise known as a spider diagram, word web or mind map. Linear notes are essentially a list and can be a convenient way of recording material, but branch notes have the advantage of being more memorable since you can incorporate icons and diagrams within them. You can use colours with both types of notes as well as print or underline words or sections that are particularly important. It's self-evident that your notes should be well spread out and systematically arranged.

If you prefer to use a listing approach you can choose a number of systems, examples of which are given below. Pick one from the examples below and stick with it. If you use more than one way of listing your points it could be confusing when you come to review the notes at a later date.

- Arabic numerals: 1, 2, 3, 4, 5, 6 . . .

- Letters: A, B, C, D, E . . . or (a), (b), (c), (d), (e) . . .

- Decimal system: 1.1, 1.2, 1.3, 1.3.1, 1.3.2, 2.1, 2.2 . . .

- Roman: I, II, III, IV, V . . . or (i), (ii), (iii), (iv), (v) . . .

- Combinations: 1   A
                  2 a)   B 1
                    b)   2
                      i)   a)
                      ii)   b)
                      iii)   c)

Branching notes, however, can give you greater organizational freedom to use all of the page and spread the notes out in a way that seems 'natural'. An example of some branch notes is given on page 125. It illustrates the information someone might jot down before deciding what further steps to take in order to avoid financial troubles following the death of their partner.

Taking notes from books or from listening to what people say can be difficult. A common mistake is to write down as much as possible just in case you miss something important. But there are clues in the words and phrases people speak and how books are organized that can help you in deciding what is useful to note and what you needn't bother with. Concentrate on the following leads, which are the bones of what someone has written or is saying:

- **Main ideas** These are often listed, and are indicated by sequencing words, such as: firstly, secondly, then, next, afterwards, finally, last of all.

- **Important points** These are points that are usually reinforced and emphasized by speakers or writers. Look out for these as they are of vital importance in helping you separate what is useful to you from what is not. Methods used for emphasis include: rephrasing the idea, underlining the significant words, or intonation.

- **Cause and effect** Relationships between two ideas are important because they can tell you the consequences of an action. These are often illustrated by the following words: therefore, thus, so, because, since.

- **Conflicting ideas** These are presented through 'linking' words or phrases such as: but, although, yet, however, on the other hand, in spite of this, nevertheless.

- **Summarizing** This is a way of concluding or drawing together the threads of an argument and especially important to keep an eye out for. It usually follows phrases such as: to sum up, in conclusion, in other words, to summarize.

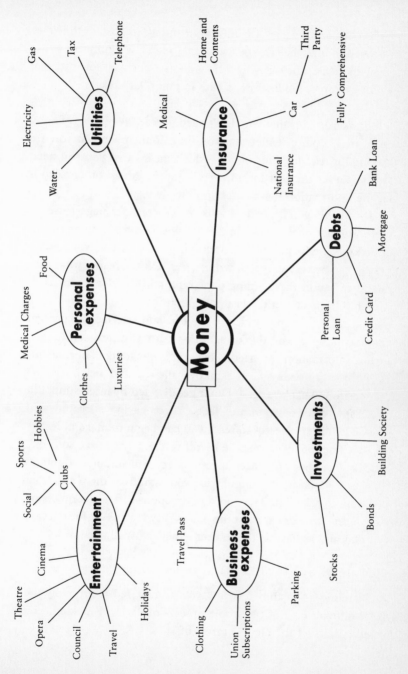

- **Examples**   These are only *detail* and it's important to realize that although they can be useful they aren't as significant as the main ideas. They usually follow phrases such as: for instance, for example, to illustrate, a case in point, let's take.

It follows from this that you don't need to read *every* word of *every* book, magazine or leaflet that you find. Remember that you are looking for *relevant* information, which means that you will need to first survey the text for an overall impression and then scan it for the information that relates specifically to you.

To do this you'll need to look at the contents page to see if there are any chapter headings that will point you in the right direction. The first and last paragraphs of any chapter you choose to read can be very useful. A writer often tells the reader what they intend to say in the opening paragraph and usually summarizes what has been said in the last paragraph.

Having got a general idea of the text and selected the general chapters or pages you think might be useful, you can scan for any further information you need. This isn't like reading in normal linear fashion. To scan, simply skim over the text and pick out information from what you read. Don't get diverted by interesting, but irrelevant, discussion of the facts. After having surveyed and scanned what you've got to read, you can begin to make notes.

As a final point, make sure that if you're going to see someone specific, like a bank manager, investment consultant, or accountant, you have a detailed account of what you want from them and what you want to ask them. Have a list of questions and take a notebook so you can write down all of the points they make. Ask for relevant booklets and leaflets on the subject – they're usually free.

Interpreting the information

Interpreting all of the facts that you've gathered is probably the most difficult part of the whole process of decision-making. You should interpret the facts in terms of:

- whether they will help you achieve your aims

- the consequences for you, and others around you, of acting on the information you've gathered

There are two main difficulties in this. The first of these is in trying to be objective and not allowing your prejudices or feelings to affect your judgement. Perhaps the only way to overcome these is to imagine that you are interpreting the information on someone else's behalf rather than for yourself. It could be for your boss, a good friend, or even a charitable organization.

The second is equally problematic. Even in the unlikely event of having every single available fact, we are simply unable to foresee *all* the possible consequences of taking any one of a number of courses of action. It is for this reason that *any* decision that you take, based on information that you have done your best to interpret as objectively as you can, *will* involve risk. Don't paralyse yourself with worry thinking about risks, continually asking yourself: 'What if? . . .' Instead, accept that you are unable to predict the future, and focus on making the best interpretation of the facts that you can.

It helps if you can write your evaluation of the facts down on paper. A *balance sheet* approach is one way of outlining all the options that you have based on the information that you've gathered, and it's especially useful if you have other people to think about. The balance sheet approach helps you look at the consequences of an action from different perspectives:

- What will be the personal gains and losses resulting from taking this course of action?

- What gains and losses will there be for other people close to me?

- What social gains and losses are there in terms of work, family, and organizations that I belong to?

Ideally, you would draw up a balance sheet for each of the *potential* decisions that face you. They can be as detailed as you want. The advantage of this method is that it will make you consider the wider issues that are encompassed by any decision you might take. Naturally, this can only help you in coming to a more balanced conclusion.

The example on page 129 illustrates how this approach can work. The context is of a woman widowed in her late forties who is planning to go back to work. That is the major decision she faces. While her husband was alive she had a job in a firm of accountants. Life insurance has provided some financial support for the family and has secured the family home, but there are still some problems in paying off business debts. She has a son and a daughter. The daughter is planning to go on to further education and the son works in a local electronics factory, but is currently living at home.

Making the decision

If you've done all the homework, you should find that the decision almost makes itself, though it doesn't do any harm to quickly re-evaluate all of the alternatives before making your choice. However, remember that once the decision is made, you've committed yourself to a course of action. It has been *your* choice and *your* responsibility. Accept this responsibility. If things don't work out just as you expected don't go blaming anyone else. Don't look back, thinking what might have been or feeling that your expectations haven't been fulfilled. The image you had of what *should* have happened as a result of your decision is irrelevant to the realities of its consequences; it's a waste of time thinking about whether you could have done it better another way.

Since we're unable to predict exactly what will happen, it's almost a complete certainty that the results of your decision will

Gains for self	Acceptable because	Not acceptable because
1. I'll have extra disposable income for the family. 2. I'll have greater self-esteem by doing something constructive.	1. The extra money will help in paying off outstanding bills; I'll be fulfilling a role as breadwinner. 2. Being active will help me feel as though I'm getting my life together.	1. The initial stresses of meeting new people may be very difficult. 2. I may have to move to a new town in the future because the company is planning to relocate some staff next year.

Losses for self	Acceptable because	Not acceptable because
1. I'll lose the time I feel I need to work through my grief.	1. I should try to become more involved in life and not allow myself to mope.	1. I think it's important for me to make sure I'm ready to start again. I don't want to rush.

Gains for others	Acceptable because	Not acceptable because
1. Starting a job will help the children realize that I'm not helpless; they'll feel less worried about me. 2. The children will take on more responsibility in looking after the house.	1. It's important that the children should feel as though they have a lead from me. 2. The children will be more independent.	1. We should be working together as a family.

Losses for others	Acceptable because	Not acceptable because
1. I'll have less time to devote to the children.	1. The children are old enough to look after themselves.	1. I'll miss out on being with the children as young adults.

Social gains	Acceptable because	Not acceptable because
1. We will have a more comfortable standard of living. 2. I will widen my circle of friends and acquaintances.	1. We need extra money not only to survive but also to enjoy life. 2. I'll have new people to know.	1. The balance of more time away from the family and the stresses of possibly having to move may not be worth the money.

Social losses	Acceptable because	Not acceptable because
1. By taking a new job the children may feel that we are less of a family unit. 2. If I have to move to a new town I might lose contact with all my old friends.	1. The children are on the point of starting their careers and will leave home soon enough.	1. I should be concentrating on building the family rather than appearing to let it fall apart. 2. I like my friends and I wouldn't want to lose touch with them.

not be perfect. But instead of cursing your 'bad' choice, look over what has happened and make any adjustments you think will improve your situation. Don't think, because you've invested time and effort in making the original decision, you should doggedly stick to what you originally intended.

eight

Looking after your health

There's evidence to suggest that the health of the elderly who have been recently bereaved is particularly at risk. Research has shown that their mortality rate can be some 40% higher than might normally be expected in the first six months following the death of a partner. Of course, there are many reasons for this, but perhaps most notable is the sense of despair and misery caused by the death of a loved one, which reduces resistance to illness and disease. There are other factors, for example, the death of a partner removes the support structure for the bereaved. They are no longer reminded to take medication regularly, eat balanced meals or make and keep doctor's or dentist's appointments.

However, there are potential health risks for everyone who has been bereaved. Mortality rates are not so significant for those bereaved at a younger age, or for those who have lost a sibling, friend, or even a child, but the hopelessness and depression associated with bereavement can cause any person to become prey to ilnesses and chronic disorders such as loss of appetite or weight, and difficulty in sleeping at night. Keeping healthy is essential in getting through the grief process. In addition to physical benefits, there are psychological and social advantages to keeping fit and healthy.

Quite simply, diet and exercise give results that make people feel good about themselves. Through recreation it's also possible to meet people and create positive feelings of social self-worth. A health programme can be invaluable in reducing the excessive stress and anxiety associated with loss and providing a solid platform for making life meaningful again. In addition, the fitter you are and the more balanced your meals are, the more energy you'll have to expend on other activities.

All of this adds up to a powerful argument which suggests that you can't afford *not* to maintain your health. It might be tempting to say 'I can't be bothered' or 'I'm just *not* going to exercise after all this trauma . . .', but any activity that helps divert your attention away from the tension and depression of loss and puts the immediate sorrowful circumstances of your life in a more positive light can only be worthwhile.

But maintaining health isn't just stopping smoking, cutting down on drinking and having more than a cup of tea or coffee for breakfast. Doing these things will help, of course, but what's really needed is a combination of nutritious food, exercise and rest. These are the three essential elements necessary to maintain good health, and if you are committed to a planned programme you'll reap the benefits in a relatively short space of time.

Nutrition

Looking at health food shops, you might imagine that all you have to do is buy some 'super' foods and miraculously improve your health and fitness. It would be extremely convenient if all we had to do was to take megadoses of vitamins, minerals, bee pollen or royal jelly, and drink 'slimming' tea, but unfortunately no amount of eating one particular kind of food or food supplement will result in improved physical fitness or mental alertness. Research has shown that none of the above has *any* value in an otherwise balanced diet and, in the case of large doses of vitamin B complex, can be harmful. Even the benefits of taking some varieties of ginseng, long the mainstay of the health food industry, have recently been questioned by scientists.

The key to good nutrition is not overloading on bran and prunes (sprinkled with lecithin), popping a couple of multi-vitamin pills and washing it all down with a pint of carrot juice; it lies in making sensible food choices from a wide range of foods in order to give your body a healthy combination of basic nutrients.

The problem is that the typical Western diet contains too much sugar, salt, fat and alcohol and not enough carbohydrates, water or dietary fibre. We eat an excessive amount of sugar in cakes, sweets and pastries that is converted to glucose and stored as fat, and leads to people being overweight and suffering coronary heart disease. The high amount of fat that the average person consumes is also a contributory factor in coronary heart disease. It can also result in increased blood pressure, diabetes, gallstones, gout and a risk of bowel or breast cancer. Excess salt, as is commonly known, can lead to dangerously high blood pressure.

Sugar

Sugar, as a nutritional category, refers to a range of carbohydrates including glucose, fructose, maltose and lactose, but for most people 'sugar' is refined, white, granulated or cube sucrose that we add to tea and coffee, and find in sweets, biscuits and soft drinks. Nutritionally, refined sugar has no value; it contains no vitamins, minerals, fibre or trace elements. Its only value is that it provides the body with calories. Because refined sugar makes things taste good we're tempted to eat too much of it at the expense of nutritious foods. Often we're unaware of how much we consume because a lot is already found in supermarket products such as breakfast cereals, desserts, cake mixes and jams.

It's very important to cut down on this redundant source of calories because any excess glucose, which is formed by the breakdown of sugars, is laid down as fat. You can do this by taking the following action:

• drink water or *pure* fruit juices instead of fizzy drinks and cordials

- cut down on cakes, biscuits, jams and confectionery

- choose fresh fruits for snacks and after meals instead of sticky sweets and desserts

- eat breakfast cereals that have no added sugar, such as porridge or homemade muesli

Salt

There's more than enough salt in food for a body's nutritional requirements. Like sugar, the main reason that people add salt to their food is because it makes it taste good, but it's often suggested that anyone who exercises needs a lot of salt because salt is excreted through sweat pores during vigorous activity. However, the amount that is lost is very small and the vast majority of people – even athletes – need no extra salt in their diet over and above that which occurs naturally in foods.

Mostly, wanting to eat more salt than is necessary is a combination of habit and poor cooking practices. So instead of reaching across the table for the salt cellar make sure that you taste everything beforehand. Be imaginative in your cooking; flavour your food with fresh herbs, and steam or stir-fry your vegetables to keep in the natural flavours and prevent the destruction of vitamins and minerals.

You can help yourself by making sensible choices at the supermarket. Look carefully at nutritional labels on the sides of packets. Many foods nowadays, such as cereals, vegetable spreads or butter, have low or reduced-salt varieties. Avoid buying processed meats like sausages, hams or corned beef that have all sorts of additives including salt; choose lean, fresh meat instead.

Fat

The thought of eating fat is repulsive to most people, but we choose to eat large amounts of it hidden in various foods every day. Over a third of the average person's intake of fat comes from foods cooked in oil, and from spreads, crisps and nuts, fast foods, biscuits, cakes and confectionery. Slightly less comes from the fat that's found in meat and meat products. Dairy products such as ice cream, cheese and milk also contribute a significant amount of fat to an average diet.

Fats are an important source of energy, but it's not healthy to eat the amounts that most people do. Unsaturated fats, in particular, are believed to be a major contributor to coronary heart disease. There are several strategies you can adopt in restricting the amount of fat that you eat:

- use only a thin scraping of butter or margarine on bread

- cut down on the amount of fried food you eat

- use polyunsaturated oils such as olive oil to cook with

- take sandwiches, a salad and fruit to work instead of going out to eat fast food for lunch

- choose low-fat salad dressings, milk and cheese instead of the full fat varieties

- eat more natural low-fat foods like vegetables, fruit, cereals, pulses and grains

- buy-low fat meats like turkey, veal or chicken instead of heavily-marbled beef or fatty pork

- don't eat so many sweets, chocolates, pastries or cakes

Alcohol

It's commonly known that too much alcohol is bad for you. Quite apart from the social distress that can occur, an excess can cause liver and brain damage. But how much is too much? A couple of units isn't harmful and may even be beneficial. This translates as two glasses of wine with your evening meal or two pints of a normal strength beer, or two measures of spirits.

However, common sense doesn't often hold with someone who has been bereaved. It can be very easy to find solace in a bottle. And it's well documented that older people living alone are at risk of drifting into alcoholism. There's even evidence to suggest that some people have a genetic disposition towards alcoholism.

The problem is that drinking alcohol can be very pleasant, but it has to be done in moderation. This can be difficult on social occasions. To cut down on your intake adopt the following approaches:

- always drink a lot of water before you drink alcohol. This will stop you treating the first drink as a thirst-quencher

- have water available on the table at mealtimes. Drink it freely

- avoid drinking alcohol at lunchtime

- drink slowly

- try low-alcohol or alcohol-free beers or wines on social occasions

Carbohydrates

Carbohydrates are divided into two categories: sugars and complex carbohydrates. They provide the body with its main source of energy. All sugars, as noted above, convert to glucose with the excess stored as fat, but fructose, or fruit sugar, in combination with the fibre found in fruit, can be regarded as a complex carbohydrate.

Complex carbohydrates are *vital* to good health and should comprise some 60% of the total calorific value of all foods you eat. This means eating more bread, pasta, potatoes, rice, oats, barley, corn, lentils, beans and peas of all types, and occasionally nuts instead of meat. As a rule choose wholemeal products wherever possible.

Water

It might seem strange to have a separate section on water when talking about nutrition, but it is so important to good health that it merits highlighting. Most people drink far too little water and it's even more important for people who start an exercise programme, to prevent dehydration through sweat loss. Even someone who does no exercise should drink about eight large glasses of water every day. Drinks like tea and coffee are no substitute for drinking water because they overload the body with caffeine and tannin and have a negative effect on the body's natural balance of liquids in much the same way as alcohol does.

If you're in doubt, check the colour of your urine. It should be almost colourless except for the morning, when it will be darker.

Fibre

Dietary fibre is the classification given to material in plant foods such as cereals, beans, grains, pulses and seeds, that is not digested by enzymes in the small intestine. Not all fibre is coarse and obviously fibrous. Some, like pectin, is water-soluble and is digested in the large intestine.

However, all fibre is essential to good health. It prevents constipation and is linked to a possible reduction in bowel cancer, diabetes, heart disease and gallstones. It's very easy to increase the amount of fibre in your diet by doing the following:

- eat more fruit and vegetables

- buy more wholegrain products

- don't remove the skin on fruit and vegetables unless it's absolutely necessary

Good nutrition should be for life and, if properly managed, will produce results that will increase your feelings of self-worth. It can also be enjoyable and diverting to plan good, nutritious meals. If you eat a wide range of foods there will be no need for you to buy vitamin or mineral supplements. Millions of pills and capsules are sold each year to people who don't need them. The best way to make sure that you're getting enough vitamins and minerals is to eat lots of fruit and vegetables, wholemeal cereals, grains and fish. Vegetarians might worry about not getting enough vitamin B12, but there are enough natural sources of this not to be a real concern.

In addition, if you're worried that you're overweight, you might consider buying a diet book. But be careful. Several popular diet books suggest that there is a short cut to balancing a diet and promoting weight loss. There are protein diets, 'food-combining' diets, fibre diets, fasting diets, fat-dissolving diets and even diets that are based on eating fat.

All of these diets, including 'crash' diets or diets that claim to make particular parts of your body slimmer, should be treated with extreme scepticism at best. Most of them rely on reducing body fluids. This results in quick 'weight' loss that cannot be sustained. When the dieter's metabolic rate adjusts, or they simply drink some water, the 'weight' is restored. Fasting diets have been proven to dangerously reduce levels of glucose and essential minerals. And there is no such thing as a food with fat-dissolving properties.

The only sensible diet is one based on balanced nutrition and an appropriate intake of calories. Make sure that you have a balance of the right kind of foods and set yourself realistic goals of losing a pound or so a week. This in itself is another way of creating positive feelings in all aspects of your self-worth. To get an idea of *what*, *when*, and *how much* you eat at the moment, use a chart like the one shown for a week to analyse your eating habits. Include drinks and snacks. Entries for Monday have been done as an example.

	Mon	Tue	Wed	Thur	Fri	Sat	Sun
AM	*Breakfast at 8:15:* 2 cups of coffee, bowl of cornflakes with milk, 2 slices of brown toast, butter & jam *Snack at 11:* banana, yoghurt & coffee						
Lunch	*Lunch:* takeaway lentil soup, bacon and tomato sandwich, can of coke & 1 Danish pastry						
PM	*Snack at 4:* 1 carton orange juice *Main meal at 7:* Pasta, tomato sauce made with capers, olives, anchovies, onions, garlic & olive oil, garlic bread, 2 glasses red wine, 2 scoops ice cream						
Evening	*Snack at 8:30 watching TV:* 1 packet low-fat crisps, coffee, mineral water *Snack before bed:* 1 glass milk						

Even from the limited information given in this example, we can see that this person hasn't eaten particularly healthily. They haven't eaten any vegetables or salad all day, and the only fresh fruit they've had is a banana. The amount of coffee they've drunk is a little excessive, and there's too much oil, fat, salt and sugar in the olive oil, ice cream, bacon, full-cream milk and crisps. The main meal has good carbohydrate content in the form of pasta, but there's insufficient intake of fibre and water.

After you've finished filling the chart in use the information to analyse your eating habits. Think about the following areas:

- Do you eat set meals at a table?

- Do you snack between meals?

- Think about the quality of the food you eat. Does it have too much sugar, salt or fat, and too little water or fibre, or insufficient complex carbohydrates?

- How much alcohol do you drink?

When you check your own eating habits you may be surprised. But be honest with yourself because you will need all the facts before you decide how you can change and improve your diet.

Exercise

The most essential element of any exercise programme is enjoyment, and certainly no-one is going to carry on from day to day and week to week with something that they regard as a chore. Exercise isn't just about improving the body. It can also help to calm the mind. And it can provide a ready-made social structure to bring you into contact with other people. This is vital to someone who has been bereaved. You can not only improve your health, but also give yourself a routine that will provide structure in your life. Exercise can be the key to rebuilding your confidence either through regaining your fitness or by achieving something you haven't attempted before.

There are innumerable forms of exercise to choose from. You might want to consider the following:

- **Exercise classes** These are perhaps the best way of combining health with social interaction. You could attend classes in such activities as aerobics, dance, aquarobics, martial arts or maybe ballet. All of these types of activity have the added benefit of being leader-directed; the participants don't need to worry about having to organize a fitness programme.

- **Team games** Many team sports provide an element of competition and are also often linked with social events. A regular game with people on a weekday evening or on a Saturday can provide a welcome way of forcing yourself to get out of the house and socialize. Examples of these kinds of activities include football, cricket, hockey, netball, volleyball.

- **Twosomes** Some people prefer the stimulus of competing one-to-one with a friend or someone who gives them a 'good game'. Tennis, squash, badminton and table tennis are favourites and, for people who are older and perhaps less fit, golf, bowls or croquet can provide an adequate amount of exercise.

- **The great outdoors** The countryside can provide all manner of activities for people of all levels of fitness and inclinations to join in with others. Ramblers' associations, hill-walking clubs, canoeing and rowing clubs are places where you can meet people and get good all-round exercise.

Of course, there are some people who prefer their own company. They don't like to depend on anyone or feel as though they're beholden to someone else. They like the freedom to arrange their time according to the way they feel. If they go swimming, cycling, walking or jogging they can go when *they* want to and not have to make an arrangement with another person.

In many ways the solitariness of such activities can be a real blessing at this difficult time. The monotony of running or swimming can be very relaxing – almost in a meditative way. It will help in releasing much of the tension that will have built up since the death of your loved one.

How much?

Naturally, you will want to do the 'right' amount of exercise. This is especially important for a more elderly person, or someone who has previously been inactive and led a sedentary lifestyle for years. Statistically, most people become widowed in middle or old age and such people can be worried about not being fit enough even to *start* an exercise programme. There is also the wear and tear of getting older to take into account. For example, rheumatoid arthritis, which results in a painful inflammation and swelling of joints, is common in late middle age; it affects women more than men. Osteoarthritis, which can also be very debilitating, is a deterioration of weight-bearing bones and occurs primarily in hips, knees and the spine.

It's true that strenuous exercise *can* have risks, but these must be weighed up against the risks of *not* exercising. In reality, the chances of a normal man suffering, say, a cardiac arrest during strenuous exercise are several million to one. The odds are much greater for women. If in doubt you should talk to your doctor before beginning any exercise programme.

However, there are a number of exercise programmes that are very suitable for older adults. A very popular one is aquarobics. These are exercises performed in water. Among the many advantages of this form of exercise is that as much as 85% of the body's weight is supported in the water, which reduces stress on joints. This is clearly beneficial for older exercisers who recognize the progressive weakening of their muscles, see restricted movement because of arthritis, and have back problems or brittle bones.

Aquarobics classes are regularly held in local swimming baths, but if you're not near a local baths an alternative would be to go on the following health walk/jog. It needs no special equipment and you can increase the pace of the different elements as you get fitter. You might feel a little self-conscious at first, but try to stick with it.

The health walk/jog

Try the following exercise, which is designed to enable you to experience the relaxation response:

1. Start from your front door and walk or jog 200 metres. Stop. Bend from the waist and *slowly* touch your toes. Do *not* bounce or stretch your tendons unnecessarily. Try to build up to ten repetitions of this exercise.

2. Walk or jog 200 metres. Stop. Put your hands on your hips and bend slowly from the waist. Keep your back straight. Return to your original position. Try to build up to ten repetitions.

3. Walk or jog 200 metres. Stop. By this time you should be warmed up and ready to do some star jumps. Try to build up to twenty repetitions. One star jump is as follows:

- start with your feet together and arms straight by your sides
- jump up and move your feet apart laterally in line with your shoulders while, at the same time, raising your arms to a horizontal position finishing at shoulder height
- jump up and bring your feet together; return your arms to their original position

4. Walk or jog 200 metres. Stop. Get down on all fours and get ready to do some press-ups. These can be difficult for some

---

people. You can make them easier by supporting yourself on your knees instead of your toes. Keep your back straight and do them slowly. Try to build up to ten repetitions.

5. Walk or jog 200 metres. Stop. Stand with your feet slightly more than shoulder width apart. Raise your arms laterally in line with your shoulders. Bend from the waist and, keeping your arms as straight as possible, touch your left foot with your right hand. Then touch your right foot with your left hand. Straighten up to your original position. Don't rush it. Try to build up to ten repetitions.

6. Walk or jog 200 metres. Stop. Stand with your feet slightly apart with your arms by your sides. Raise your arms laterally, bending at the elbow. Slowly push your elbows back as far as possible. You might feel a bit like a demented chicken, but you will also be exercising your upper back. Try to build up to ten repetitions.

7. Walk or jog 200 metres. Stop. Find a tree or wall and lean against it at an angle with one leg stretched back to support you at the rear and the other placed in front to support your body. Each foot should be pointing towards the wall or tree. Push against it for a count of ten. Relax. Swap the position of your feet. Push once more. Try to build up to ten repetitions.

8. Walk or jog 200 metres. Stop. Stand straight with your arms by your sides. Try to press your arms into your body for a count of ten. Relax. Try to build up to ten repetitions.

9. Walk or jog 200 metres. Stop. Put the palms of your hands together. Raise them to your chest. Press them hard together for a count of ten. Relax. Try to build up to ten repetitions.

10. Walk or jog the remaining distance to the front door of your house or flat.

If you're slightly fitter you could add some sit-ups, but remember that these can be bad for the back and so, if in doubt, don't push it. As a rule, the minimum number of times you should exercise is three or four times a week, during which you should raise your heart rate to 75% of its maximum capacity for 20–30 minutes. You can roughly estimate your maximum heart rate by subtracting your age from 220. So, if you are fifty years of age, your maximum heart rate will be around 170 beats per minute; try to keep your heart beating at around 130 beats for the duration of the exercise period.

However, don't feel that you are obliged to achieve this level *every* time you go out and exercise. You can't motivate yourself to work at optimum levels each time you exercise. Think about the following guidelines when you're trying to get yourself fitter:

- **Take it easy once in a while**   One of the most elementary mistakes that people make in starting an exercise programme is believing that they have to jog, play tennis, swim or walk as hard, if not harder, from one day to the next without any let-up. This isn't true. Make sure that you have the *occasional* easy day where you work to, say, 40% of your capacity. By doing this you'll give your body the chance to recover and when you come to your next exercise session, you'll be able to enjoy it all the more. Remember that the aim is to enjoy the exercise and not recreate the miserable enforced activity that you might have experienced at school.

- **Don't go out and exercise just because it's on your programme**   An exercise schedule is a guide and nothing more. Don't be a slave to it. If it's howling outside don't feel that you have to go out and run or walk to the gym, because you'll just end up hating it. Of course, don't use this as an excuse. Be honest with yourself and only cancel a session if it's *really* necessary.

- **Exercise is for enjoyment** The intended outcome of improving your health is to enhance the quality of your life; it's a way of beginning to understand that life can become meaningful again. Any activity that you choose to take up is only *part* of your whole life plan. It's important to avoid becoming over-motivated to the point of developing a negative addiction, and exercising too much at the expense of other things in your life. This can be harmful in much the same way that over- or under-eating can be harmful.

- **Relaxation is the key** Try to avoid going to the pool, the gym, the squash courts or the mountains when everyone else goes. Granted, this can be difficult because most people have the same hours off, such as lunchtimes, straight after work or at weekends, but try to choose your times carefully. If you like running, map out an interesting route away from traffic and roads. It can make an enormous difference to your state of mind knowing that you don't have to worry about distractions.

Rest

It can be very difficult for someone who has been bereaved to sleep. The stresses of the present and anxieties for the future make it extremely hard for them to rest easy at night. This lack of adequate sleep in itself is, of course, a stress factor that has to be eliminated because a gradual build-up of stress will inevitably cause further worry and anxiety which will lead to still more of a lack of rest.

This viscious circle has to be broken. The way *not* to do this is by taking sleeping pills or by having a couple of whiskies to induce sleep. This will only add to your problems in the long run. Instead, there are a few sensible and practical steps that you can take which will help in giving you a good night's rest:

- avoid drinking caffeinated drinks such as coffee, tea or some carbonated drinks before you go to bed

- make sure that your bedroom is restful to sleep in – not too noisy or too light – and that your bed is comfortable

- keep busy during the day by working and exercising so that you are ready for sleep at night

It's also possible to train yourself to relax before going to bed. There are various methods you can use in order to achieve this, including meditation or self-suggestion, techniques for which can be found in Chapter 5. These aim to help you in preventing worry, depression and anxiety, which rob you of the rest you need at this time.

There may well be times, however, when you just can't sleep. Be prepared for this. Try to stop yourself from simply lying in bed missing your loved one and slipping into despair. If you can, get up and do something useful such as writing a letter you've been meaning to write to for some time, or writing out a plan for what you're going to do this coming day. If you're good with your hands you could get up and fix that leaking tap you've been meaning to fix for a while. Perhaps you could do some washing or ironing if there's any that needs attending to. Or you could just read a book or listen to the radio.

If, despite all the steps you're taking, you find that you simply are unable to get to sleep, then consult your doctor. He or she may be able to provide additional practical help to ensure that you get a peaceful night's sleep.

Conclusion

Most people who have been bereaved find out fairly early on that those who *haven't* have great difficulty in understanding how the bereaved think. In addition, bereavement and grief can be frightening because of the intense feeling they unleash. At times, this can make the already private nature of reorganizing your life a wearying and solitary task. But coming to terms with the certainty of our own death, even though it may have been through the distress of losing a loved one, is a great comfort.

It *is* possible to cope with fears and feelings and, ironically, in some ways emerge stronger than you were before your loved one died. Many people will notice this and will say that they 'admire you' for having responded 'so well' to your circumstances. And maybe it's true – someone who has been bereaved is probably more capable of dealing with many of life's crises than someone who hasn't been through the same experience. But just because you may have come through what could turn out to be the worst ordeal of your life, it doesn't mean that you will be able to face further experiences of loss without pain.

Surviving a death leaves a wound that is all too easily opened up again. Instead of being able to rationalize and withstand the agony of someone else's grief, you may find that you've developed a heightened sensitivity to death and dying. This has certainly been my experience. Since Shirin's death other people close to me have died, which on each occasion resurrected the acute pain I felt when she was separated from me.

Nonetheless, this understanding of pain can help when people close to you are themselves bereaved. Of course, it can be difficult to know what to do. There is always the feeling that perhaps your experiences will not be relevant to anyone else, and that you might intrude on someone's private grief, especially if you were not *very* close to the family. This is not necessarily the case. You can make an enormous difference on a practical level.

Helping others grieve

It's best to be totally spontaneous with others who have been bereaved, and offer your support and condolences without reservation. Your support should be given wholeheartedly and consistently since to do otherwise will cause upset and offence. The following practical steps are worth considering:

- Visit the bereaved's home as soon as possible. Don't be timid. You may not be invited in, but the gesture will be appreciated. If you *do* go to visit someone after a death, be prepared to face tears. Be sensitive: give them every opportunity to talk about their loved one and avoid giving them advice for the future (however sensible) since this will be the last thing they will want to think about at this time. If you *can't* visit, phone.

- If the bereaved person is on their own, ask them to stay over with you for a night or two. They may well refuse, but an offer of support of this kind, genuinely meant, is very uplifting; it's a reminder that there are people thinking about them.

- Remember that people who are in shock find it difficult to plan even for the next few hours. One of the most thoughtful and helpful things you can do is make sure that there is enough food in the house. I remember one of my mother-in-law's friends turning up very soon after Shirin died with enough meals for everyone for a week, which she then put in the freezer. You might also consider inviting the bereaved over for a simple meal.

- Offer to buy anything the bereaved person needs when you go shopping. There will always be some small items that will be needed for the house.

- Take some flowers and perhaps a vase to put them in. Flowers will help the family to realize that even though they are in anguish, life is still beautiful.

Your own death

Inevitably, and especially if you have suffered a bereavement in later life, you will have begun to think more about your *own* mortality, started to re-evaluate your *own* relationships and begun to re-organize your affairs in preparation for your *own* death. Much of this preparation will involve legal documentation such as making a will or renegotiating insurance for surviving partners, family or loved ones.

But, there is more to preparing for death than writing a will and settling differences between yourself and others. It also involves a close look at the *processes* and possible *circumstances* surrounding death. These would include the possibility of dying in pain, the fear of dying alone, possible loss of dignity, lack of control, and aspects of medical care and spiritual needs. It is not death that people fear most, it is the period leading up to it.

While it might seem somewhat morbid, it's essential to assert your rights as death approaches. These include the following:

- You have the right to be treated as a living human being until the moment of your death.

- You have the right to participate in *all* decisions that affect your care.

- You have the right to be informed about all positive *and* negative outcomes of any treatment given to you.

- You have the right to have *all* of your questions about your care and health answered openly, honestly and non-judgementally.

- You have the right to continued expert medical and nursing care, whether your needs are for a cure or for freedom from pain.

- You have the right to sensitive and compassionate medical and nursing care in a spirit of faith, trust and optimism.

- You have the right to spiritual and emotional support as you face your death.

- You have the right to express your feelings and emotions about your approaching death in a manner that seems appropriate to you.

- You have the right to die with dignity.

- You have the right to have support for your family and loved ones after your death.

The future

Sadly, you will *have* to face the future without your loved one. This is hard. But, in time, life will be good and meaningful. It may take a year, two years, or even more, but it *will* happen – if you want it to. Although it may be little consolation at the moment if you are very recently bereaved, there is another side to surviving a death. The transition from extreme grief to adjustment brings an awareness and acceptance of the role that death plays in our lives. This knowledge of death-in-life is an important and on-going process, and can lead to a better understanding of how to live our lives.

Death is a natural process. However, the subject of death is often taboo in Western societies, and tends to be perceived almost entirely negatively. An interest in death is usually considered unnecessary and unwholesome. But attitudes to anything – including death – should be neither entirely negative nor entirely positive. Perhaps we should cultivate a greater acceptance of death as part of everyday life. A more healthy and open attitude towards it would allow us to prepare more readily for our own death because, in anticipating it, we would be able to act out better the social and personal roles that are associated with death, dying and bereavement. In this way, we might learn to appreciate each day a little bit more despite our loss, and learn to love life again.

Bibliography

Aiken County Coroner's Office. 1996. *The Coroner's Office.* http://www.aiken.net/erad/acco/index.html.

Albery, N., G. Elliot and J. Elliot. 1993. *The Natural Death Handbook.* London: Natural Death Centre.

Attewell, D. 1997. 'Life after Caroline'. *Company* Vol. 20/5, pp. 66-69.

Barbus, A. 1975. 'The dying person's bill of rights'. *American Journal of Nursing* Vol. 1/99. In Hayslip, B and P. E. Panek. 1993. *Adult Development and Aging,* p. 493.

Benson, H. 1976. *The Relaxation Response.* New York: Avon Books.

Bertman, S. L. 1991. *Facing Death: Images, Insights, and Interventions.* Bristol, PA: Taylor & Francis

Bohannon, J. R. 1990–1991. 'Grief responses following the death of a child: A longitudinal study'. *Omega* Vol. 10, pp. 145–158.

Burns, R. B. 1992. *10 Skills for Working with Stress.* Chatswood NSW: Business and Professional Publishing.

Cahill, R. J. 1996. *Report by the Chief Coroner of the Australian Capital Territory to the Attorney General of the Australian Capital Territory 1 July 1995 to June 1996.*
http://actag.canberra.edu.au/actag/Reports/Dept/ar/1996/47.html.

Caine, L. 1974. *Widow.* New York: William Morrow.

Calhoun, L. G., J. W. Selby and M. E. Faulstich. 1982. 'Reactions of the parents to the child suicide: A study of social impressions'. *Journal of Consulting and Clinical Psychology* Vol. 48, pp. 535–536.

Carnegie, D. 1984. *How to Stop Worrying and Start Living*. New York: Simon and Schuster.

Cummings, E. and W. E. Henry. 1961. *Growing Old: The Process of Disengagement*. New York: Basic Books.

Department of Social Security and the Central Office of Information. 1990. *What to do after a death: A guide to what you must do and the help you can get. Leaflet D49*. London: DSS.

Dodd, B. 1991. 'Bereavement'. In Cochrane, R. and D. Carroll (eds.) *Psychology and Social Issues*. London: The Falmer Press.

Eggar, G. and N. Champion. 1990. (2nd edn.) *The Fitness Leader's Handbook*. Kenthurst: Kangaroo Press.

Ellis, A. 1977. 'Rational emotive therapy'. *Cognitive Psychology* Vol. 7, pp. 2–42.

Fontana, D. 1991. *The Elements of Meditation*. Shaftesbury: Element.

Gill, S. and J. Fox. 1996. *The Dead Good Funerals Book*. Ulverstone, UK: Engineers of the Imagination.

Glasser, W. 1976. *Positive Addiction*. New York: Harper and Row.

Goode, W. J. 1964. *The Family*. Englewood Cliffs, NJ: Prentice-Hall.

Harris, B. G. 1986. 'Induced abortion'. In Rando, T. (ed.) *Parental Loss of a Child* pp. 241–256 Champaign, IL: Research Press.

Hawton, K. 1986. *Suicide and Attempted Suicide Among Children and Adolescents*. London: Sage Publications Ltd.

Hayslip, B. and P. E. Panek. 1993. *Adult Development and Aging*. New York: Harper Collins.

Hetherington, E. M. 1979. 'Divorce: A child's perspective'. *American Psychologist*. Vol. 34, pp. 851–858.

Heyman, D. K. and D. T. Gianturco. 1973. 'Long-term adaptation by the elderly to bereavement'. *Journal of Gerontology* Vol. 28, pp. 359–62.

Holmes, J. H. and R. H. Rahe. 1967. 'The social readjustment rating scale'. *Journal of Personality and Social Psychology* Vol. 11, pp. 213–218.

Humphry, D. 1995. 'Why I believe in voluntary euthanasia: The case for rational suicide'.
http://www.rights.org/~deathnet/Humphry_essay.html.

Hutton, D. 1997. 'A good death'. *Vogue* Vol. 163/5, pp. 160–161, 202.

Jacobsen, E. 1938. *Progressive Relaxation*. Chicago: University of Chicago Press.

Jagadish, K. R. I. 1992. *Health and Yoga Through Diet*. Singapore: Ang Publications.

Jeffers, S. 1991. *Feel the Fear and Do it Anyway*. London: Arrow.

Kalish, R. 1976. 'Death and dying in a social context'. In Binstock, R. and E. Shanas (eds.) *Handbook of Aging and the Social Sciences* pp. 149–172. New York: Van Nostrand Reinhold.

Kastenbaum, R. 1986. *Death, Society and Human Experience*. Columbus, OH: Merrill.

Kimmel, D. C. 1990 (3rd edn.). *Adulthood and Aging*. New York: John Wiley & Sons.

Kübler-Ross, E. 1975. *Questions and Answers on Death and Dying*. New York: Macmillan.

Lichtenberg, S. 1990. 'Remembering Becky'. *Omega* Vol. 21, pp. 83–89.

Lloyd, A. 1982. *Easing Grief for Oneself and for Other People*. Walton-on-Thames: Relaxation for Living.

Lopata, H. Z. 1975. *Widowhood in an American City*. Cambridge: Schenkman.

Mandelbaum, D. G. 1959. 'Social uses of funeral rites'. In Feifel (ed.) *The Meaning of Death*. pp. 198–217. New York: McGraw-Hill.

McKay, M., M. Davis and P. Fanning. 1983. *Messages: The Communication Skills Book*. Oakland CA: New Harbinger Publications.

Miller, M. 1982. 'Surviving the loss of a loved one: An inside look at grief counseling'. In J. A. Freuhling (ed.), *Source Book on Death and Dying*. pp. 189–192. Chicago: Marquis Professional Publications.

National Funeral Director's Association. 1996. *Marketplace; Consumer education series brochures.*
http://www.nfda.org/resources/marketplace/brochures/arrange.html.

No author. 1995. *Indiana Code 23-14-31-27.*
http://www.law.indiana.edu/codes/in/23/23-14-31-27.html

No author. 1996. *Completing Funeral Arrangements.*
http://www.emedia.com.au/chippers/Funeral Arrangements. html#registration

Office of Revisor of Statutes, State of Minnesota. 1996. *Minnesota Statutes 1996; 13.83 Medical examiner data.*
http://www.revisor.leg.state.mn.us/st96/13/83.html

Orange County Sheriff-Coroner Department. 1997. *Primary Duties of the Coroner.*
http://www.ocsd.org/duties.html

Parkes, C. M. 1987 (2nd edn.). *Bereavement: Studies in Adult Life.* Madison, CT: International Universities Press.

Peterson, J. A. 1980. 'Social-psychological aspects of death and dying and metal health'. In Birren, J. E. and R. B. Sloane (eds.) 1980. *Handbook of Mental Health and Aging.* Englewood Cliffs, NJ: Prentice-Hall.

Rando, T. A. (ed.) 1986. *Loss and Anticipatory Grief.* Lexington, MA: Lexington Books

Rogers, D. 1986 (3rd edn.). *The Adult Years: An Introduction to Aging.* Englewood Cliffs, NJ: Prentice-Hall.

Rowland, K. 1977. 'Environmental events predicting death for the elderly'. *Psychological Bulletin* Vol. 84, pp. 349–372.

Schulz, R. 1978. *The Psychology of Death, Dying and Bereavement.* Reading, MA: Addison-Wesley.

Share, L. 1978. 'Family communication in the crisis of a child's fatal illness: A literature review and analysis'. In Kalish, R. *Caring for the Dying and the Bereaved.* Farmingdale, NY: Baywood.

Smolak, L. 1993. *Adult Development.* London: Prentice Hall.

Stokes, G. 1992. *On Being Old: The Psychology of Later Life.* London: The Falmer Press.

Stroebe, W. and M. Stroebe. 1987. *Bereavement and Health: The Psychological and Physical Consequences of Partner Loss*. New York: Cambridge.

Thomas, S. 1996. 'How to deal with life after death'. *Chic* Vol. 1/8, pp. 28–31.

Toop, D. 1996. 'The after life'. *Vogue* Vol. 162/11, pp. 190–191, 262.

Wallace, M. J. 1980. *Study Skills in English*. Cambridge: Cambridge University Press.

Ward, B. 1993. *Good Grief*. London: Jessica Kingsley Publishers.

Westmoreland, P. 1996. 'Coping with death: Helping students grieve'. *Childhood Education: Infancy Through Adolescence* Vol 72/3, pp. 152–163.

Wischnia, B. 1995. 'Rules of the road'. *Runner's World* Vol. 30/12, pp 24–27.

Woods, R. T. and P. G. Britton. 1985. *Clinical Psychology with the Elderly*. London: Croom Helm.

Worden, J. W. 1991. (2nd edn.) *Grief Counseling and Grief Therapy: A Handbook for the Mental Health Practitioner*. New York: Springer.

Resources

Further reading

The following list of publications is grouped, approximately, by subject. In the main, the titles are self-explanatory, but I've added notes where appropriate.

General

Ainsworth-Smith, I. and P. Speck. 1982. *Letting Go: Caring for the Dying and Bereaved*. SPCK.

Bailey, A. 1985. *Death: The Great Adventure*. Lucis Press.

Boston, S. and R. Trezise. 1987. *Merely Mortal: Coping with Dying, Death and Bereavement*. Methuen.

Bowlby, J. 1980. *Loss, Sadness and Depression*. Penguin. In this book, children and the loss of a mother are the central theme.

Buckman, R. 1990. *I Don't Know What To Say: How to Help and Support Someone Who is Dying*. Macmillan Papermac. Rob Buckman is a medical doctor who has produced an accessible and practical text for the family and friends of a loved one who is facing terminal illness.

Carlson, L. 1897. *Caring For Your Own Dead.* Upper Access.

Dickenson, D. and M. Johnson (eds). 1993. *Death, Dying and Bereavement.* Sage. This is a collection of different authors' attitudes to death, and how death affects people on a human level.

Doyle, D. 1983. *Coping with a Dying Relative.* Macdonald.

Enright, D. J. (ed). 1987. *The Oxford Book of Death,* Oxford University Press.

Grollman, E. 1970. *Talking About Death.* Beacon Press. This book is intended to be read by a bereaved parent and child together.

Hastings, D. 1989. *Crisis Point: A Survivor's Guide to Living.* Macmillan Papermac.

Hinton, J. 1972. *Dying.* Penguin.

Illingworth, M. 1992. *How to Direct Your Own Funeral.* Bookstall Publications.

Jones, M. 1988. *Secret Flowers: Mourning and the Adaptation to Loss.* Women's Press. A personal account of one woman's experiences before and after the death of her husband from cancer.

Knapp, R. J. 1986. *Beyond Endurance: When a Child Dies.* Schocken Books.

Kohner, N. and P. Mares. 1991. *Who Cares Now? Caring For an Older Person.* BBC Education.

Krementz, J. 1986. *How it Feels When a Parent Dies*. Gollancz. A collection of personal accounts of eighteen children who have lost a parent.

Lake, T. 1984. *Living With Grief*. Sheldon Press. The author, a medical doctor, provides practical advice on coping with grief.

Manning, D. 1984. *Don't Take My Grief Away: What to do when you lose a loved one*. Harper & Row.

Morgan, E. 1990. *Dealing Creatively with Death*. Barclay House.

Owens, R. G. and F. Naylor. 1989. *Living While Dying: What to Do and What to Say When You Are, or Someone Close to You, is Dying*. Thorsons.

Sanders, C. 1992. *Surviving Grief and Learning to Live Again*. John Wiley & Sons.

Schiff, H. S. 1979. *The Bereaved Parent*. Souvenir Press.

Staudacher, C. 1988. *Beyond Grief: A Guide to Recovering From the Death of a Loved One*. Condor.

Staudacher, C. 1991. *Men and Grief: A Guide for Men Surviving the Death of a Loved One*. New Harbinger. In this book, Carol Saudacher describes the particular problems that men might have to face after the death of a loved one, and as in her earlier text, *Beyond Grief*, she provides a practical programme for the successful resolution of grief.

Wells, R. 1988. *Helping Children Cope with Grief: Facing a Death in the Family*. Sheldon Press.

White, J. 1988. *A Practical Guide to Death and Dying*. Quest.

Professional

Aiken, L. R. (3rd edn.) 1994. *Dying, Death, and Bereavement.* Allyn & Bacon. This text reviews and compares social scientific studies of death, and includes details on cultural, moral and other ethical issues. It has material on death and dying, widowhood, euthanasia, and abortion as loss.

Cook, A. S., and D. S. Dworkin. 1992. *Helping the Bereaved: Therapeutic Interventions for Children, Adolescents, and Adults.* Basic Books. The main thrust of the text is that each case should be treated on an individual basis with particular reference to the bereaved's cultural background.

Green, J. and M. Green. 1992. *Dealing with Death.* Chapman & Hall. This is a fairly comprehensive text that deals with practical legal issues surrounding death as well as religious needs of the bereaved.

Hockey, J. 1990. *Experiences of Death: An Anthropological Account.* Edinburgh University Press.

Jarratt, C. J. (revd. edn.). 1994. *Helping Children Cope with Separation and Loss.* Harvard Common Press. Although the primary focus of this text is not death (it deals with other issues of loss including adoption, abandonment and divorce), it does discuss practical activities intended to help a child understand loss, and to cope with strong emotions at a time of loss.

Kübler-Ross, E. 1973. *On Death and Dying.* Tavistock Publications. A seminal text on the processes involved in death and dying. The work of Elisabeth Kübler-Ross in the late 1960s has almost certainly produced a more humane attitude towards the care of the dying, and while the detail of her theories may now be open to question or suffer from rigid interpretation by others, there's no doubting the importance of her work as being pivotal to the development of bereavement intervention practice.

Kübler-Ross, E. (ed). 1975. *Death: The Final Stage of Growth*. Spectrum.

Kübler-Ross, E. 1982. *Living with Death and Dying*. Souvenir Press.

Kübler-Ross, E. 1985. *On Children and Death*. Collier Books.

LaGrand, L. E. 1986. *Coping with Separation and Loss as a Young Adult*. Charles Thomas.

Littlewood, J. 1992. *Aspects of Grief: Bereavement in Adult Life*. Routledge. A research text that addresses relatives' and society's attitude towards those who have been bereaved.

Murray, P. C. (3rd edn.). 1996. *Bereavement: Studies of Grief in Adult Life*. Routledge. An important work which is the result of twelve years' research with widows. Essential for professional counsellors.

Neuberger, J. and J. White (eds). 1991. *A Necessary End: Attitudes to Death*. Macmillan Papermac.

Rando, T. A. 1993. *Treatment of Complicated Mourning*. Research Press. Therese Rando is prolific in this field, and in this text has produced an integrated model of six phases and processes of bereavement, building on her own work and the recent finds of other researchers. Another significant text.

Rosen, E. J. 1990. *Families Facing Death: Family Dynamics of Terminal Illness*. Lexington Books.

Saunders, C. 1990. *Hospice and Palliative Care: An Interdisciplinary Approach*. Edward Arnold.

Stedeford, A. 1988. *Facing Death: Patients, Families and Professionals*. Heinemann.

Wertheimer, A. 1991. *A Special Scar: The Experiences of People Bereaved by Suicide*. Routledge. As the title suggests, this is a book aimed at an understanding of family dynamics after the loss of a loved one through suicide.

Spiritual

Benn, J. (ed). 1986. *Memorials: An Anthology of Poetry and Prose*. Ravette.

Harding, D. 1988. *The Little Book of Life and Death*. Arkana.

Mabey, J. 1988. *Words to Comfort, Words to Heal: Poems and Meditations for those who Grieve*. Oneworld Publications.

Levine, S. 1990. *Healing into Life and Death*. Gateway Books. Stephen Levine has produced several books with a spiritual slant on death, incorporating an Eastern philisophical approach. This text includes a number of meditation exercises intended to help the reader find peace and relaxation.

Rinpoche, S. 1992. *The Tibetan Book of Living and Dying*. Rider.

Wilkins, R. 1990. *The Fireside Book of Death*. Robert Hale.

Willson, J. W. 1989. *Funerals Without God: A Practical Guide to Non-Religious Funerals*. British Humanist Association.

Groups that can offer support

United Kingdom

Age Concern. Astral House, 1268 London Road, London SW16 4EJ.

Alder Centre. Royal Liverpool Children's NHS Trust, Eaton Road, Liverpool L12 2AP.
The Alder Centre can provide practical counselling for parents who have lost a child, and may also be able to put you in touch with others who have suffered such a loss.

Alzheimer's Disease Society. 158–160 Balham High Road, London SW12 913N.

Asian Family Counselling Service. 12 Lancaster Road, Southall UB1 1NW.

Association for Children with Lifethreatening Conditions and their Families (ACT). Institute of Child Health, Royal Hospital for Sick Children, St Michael's Hill, Bristol BS2 8BJ.

CALL Centre (Cancer Aid and Listening Line). Swan Buildings, 20 Swan St, Manchester M4 5JW. Tel: 0161 835 2586. CALL is a support group for cancer patients and their families.

Carers' National Association. 29 Chilworth Mews, London W2 3RG.

Child Death Helpline. Tel: 0171 829 8685.

Compassionate Friends. 53 North Street, Bristol BS3 1EN.
The Compassionate Friends are a nationwide group that can

provide a befriending service for those who have been bereaved.

Cot Death Society. 116 Alt Road, Formby, Merseyside L37 8BW.

Cot Death Research and Support for Bereaved Parents. 8a Alexandra Parade, Weston Super Mare.

CRUSE-Bereavement Care. Cruse House, 126 Sheen Road, Richmond, Surrey TW9 1UR.
CRUSE is a national organization that can put you in touch with trained carers and counsellors as well as provide advice to anyone who has suffered a bereavement. It produces a number of its own publications.

Elisabeth Kübler-Ross Foundation. PO Box 212, London NW8 7NW.

Funeral Ombudsman. 31 Southampton Row, London WC1B 5HJ.

Hospice Information Service. St. Christopher's Hospice, 51–59 Lawrie Park Road, Sydenham, London SE26 6DZ.

Lesbian and Gay Bereavement Project. Vaughan M. Williams Centre, Colindale Hospital, London NW9 5GJ.

London Association of Bereavement Services. 68 Chalton Street, London NW1.

London Lighthouse. 111–117 Lancaster Road, London W11 1QT. Tel: 071 792 1200.
The London Lighthouse is an organization for AIDS patients. It can provide guidance on funerals and memorials.

Memorial Advisory Bureau. 139 Kensington High St, London W8 6SX.

Miscarriage Association. Clayton Hospital, Northgate, Wakefield WF1 3JP.

National Association of Bereavement Services. 20 Norton Folgate, London E1 6DB.

National Association of Funeral Directors. 618 Warwick Road, Solihull, West Midlands B91 1AA.

National Association of Widows. 54–57 Allison Street, Digbeth, Birmingham B5 5TH.

National Black Bereavement Foundation. 25 Baysharn St, Camden, London NW1.

Parents of Murdered Children Support Group. 92 Corbett Tay Road, Upminster, Essex RM14 2BA.

Rainbow Centre. 27 Lilymead Avenue, Bristol, BS4 2BY.
The Centre offers counselling for children and families facing terminal illness.

Rainbow Trust. Rainbow House, 47 Eastwick Drive, Great Bookham, Surrey KT23 3PU.
This organization will give help to terminally ill children and their families.

React. 73 Whitehall Park Road, London W4 3NB.
This group can give money and equipment for terminally ill children, but note that any application must be made through a doctor or other professional party.

Samaritans. 17 Uxbridge Road, Slough, SL1 1SN.
The Samaritans provide confidential support for those in depair or near suicide. Check your telephone directory for the local number.

Shadow of Suicide (SOS). 6 Denmark St, Bristol BS1 5DQ.
SOS is a group that offers support to families of a loved one who has taken their own life.

Starlight Foundation. 8a Bloomsbury Square, London WC1A 2LP.
This is an organization that tries to grant the wishes of critically ill children.

Stillbirth and Neonatal Death Society (SANDS). 28 Portland Place, London W1N 4DE.

Terence Higgins Trust. 52–54 Grays Inn Road, London WC1X 8JU.
The Terence Higgins Trust is a charity that can give information and advice to AIDS patients and people with HIV infection.

Twins and Multiple Births Association: Bereavement Support Group. PO Box 30, Little Sutton, South Wirral L66 1TH.

War Pensions Branch. DSS Norcross, Blackpool FY5 3TA.

Australia

National SIDS Council of Australia Ltd. 357 Burnwood Road, Hawthorn, Victoria 3122. Tel/Fax: (03) 9819 9277.

SANDS (Vic). C-19 Canterbury Road, Camberwell, Victoria 3124. Tel: (03) 882 1590.
This is an organization run by volunteers to help parents who have suffered the miscarriage, stillbirth or neonatal death of their child.

Sudden Infant Death Research Foundation Inc. 1227 Malvern Road, Malvern, Victoria 3144. Tel: (03) 9822 9611 Fax: (03) 9822 2995.

Sudden Infant Death Association (NSW) Inc. 2 Harold Street, North Parramatta, NSW 2151. Tel: (02) 630 0099 Fax: (02) 630 0440.

Lifeline
Lifeline is a 24-hour national telephone crisis-counselling service. Telephone 13 1114 at the cost of a local call to be connected with the nearest of the 38 centres throughout Australia.

USA

AMEND (Aiding a Mother and Father Experiencing Neonatal Death. 1559 Ville Rosa, Hazelwood, MO 63042. Tel: (314) 291 0892.
AMEND is run by trained volunteer counsellors who have all experienced the trauma of neonatal death.

American Self-Help Clearing House. Northwest Convent Medical Center, Denville, New Jersey 07834-22995. Tel: (201) 625 9565 Fax: (201) 625 8848.
An information service that provides information on worldwide bereavement support groups, and gives advice to people interested in starting new self-help groups.

CLIMB (Center for Loss in Multiple Birth). P.O. Box 1064, Palmer, Alaska 99645. Tel: (907) 746 6123.
This is an organization that can offer phone or mail support, and specialized articles to parents who have lost multiple birth children.

Compassionate Friends. P.O. Box 3696, Oak Brook, Illinois 60522-3696. Tel: (708) 990 0010 Fax: (708) 990 0246.

The Compassionate Friends is an international support group primarily for bereaved parents and siblings.

Concerns of Police Survivors, Inc. (COPS). COPS National Office, P.O Box 3199, Camdenton, Missouri 65020. Tel: (573) 346 4911 Fax: (573) 346 1414.

COPS has a national network of support groups for the families and friends of police officers who have been killed in the line of duty. In addition to advice and support, the national office contacts surviving families at least six times each year with news and information.

Dougy Center. 3903 S.E. 52nd Avenue, P.O. Box 86582, Portland, Oregon 97286. Tel: (503) 775 5683.

The Dougy Center is devoted to helping children through the grieving process. It trains all its own staff for affiliated programmes.

In Loving Memory. 1416 Green Run Lake, Reston, Virginia 22090. Tel: (703) 435 0608.

This is primarily an information service group for bereaved parents, but in addition holds an annual conference for Bereaved Parents With No Surviving Children.

National Organization of Parents of Murdered Children. 100 East Street, B-41, Cincinnati, Ohio 45202. Tel: (513) 721 5683.

POMC offers emotional support through self-help groups, practical legal advice, and can put you in touch with professionals fully aware of the particular problems faced by parents and others who have lost a loved one through murder.

National SHARE Office (Pregnancy and Infant Loss Support Inc.). St. Joseph Health Center, 300 First Capitol Drive, St. Charles, Missouri 63301-2893. Tel: (800) 821 6819 Fax: (314) 947 7486.

The national office has details of over 100 chapters, and can offer information and support for bereaved parents and siblings.

National Sudden Infant Death Syndrome Resource Center.
2070 Chain Bridge Road, Suite 450, Vienna, VAA 22182. Tel:
(703) 821 8955 Fax: (703) 821 2098.

Pregnancy and Infant Loss Center. 1421 East Wayzata
Boulevard, Suite #30, Wayzata, Minnesota 55391. Tel: (612)
473 9372 Fax: (612) 473 8978.

Ray of Hope, Inc. P.O. Box 2323, Iowa City, Iowa 52244. Tel:
(319) 337 9890.
This is a national self-help organization for those touched by
another's suicide.

Society of Military Widows. 5535 Hempstead Way,
Springfield, VA 22151. Tel: (703) 750 1342 ext. 3007 Fax:
(703) 354 4380.
A National organization that serves the interests of women whose
husbands died on active duty or after retiring from the armed forces.

Sudden Infant Death Syndrome Alliance (SIDS Alliance).
1314 Bedford Avenue, Suite 210, Baltimore, Maryland 212208.
Tel: (410) 653 8826/(800) 221-SIDS Fax: (410) 659 8709.
This national office can give you the contact for your nearest local
affiliated chapter which can offer one-to-one support as well as
provide information and guidance on SIDS.

TAPS (Tragedy Assistance Program for Survivors, Inc.).
2001 S Street, NW, Suite 300, Washington, DC 20009. Tel:
(800) 959-TAPS Fax: (907) 274 8277.
TAPS provides a free support service specifically for families and
friends of military service personnel who have died.

THEOS (They Help Each Other Spiritually). 717 Liberty Avenue,
1301 Clark Building, Pittsburgh, PA 15222. Tel: (412) 471 7779.
THEOS is a national organization that uses mutual self-help to assist

widows of all ages and their families after the death of a loved one.

To Live Again. PO Box 415, Springfield, PA 19064. Tel: (010) 353 7740.
This support group puts you in touch with others who have lost their partners to help you though the grief process.

Twinless Twins Support Group International. 11220 St. Joe Road, Fort Wayne, IN 46835-9737. Tel: (219) 627 5414 Fax: (219) 627 5414.
This is a group that provides for the special needs of surviving twins (and others of multiple births) who have suffered the loss of a sibling.

Unite, Inc. 7600 Central Avenue, Philadelphia PA 19111-2499. Tel: (215) 728 3777.
A support group for miscarraige, neonatal and infant death. There is a fee to join the national office, but none for attending local support groups.

Widowed Person's Service. 601 E Street NW, Washington, DC 20049. Tel: (202) 434 2260.
WPS is a volunteer-run group that sends trained workers into the community to support the newly-widowed.

Canada

Bereaved Families of Ontario (BFO). 562 Eglington Avenue East, Suite 401, Toronto, Ontario M4P 1P1. Tel: (416) 440 0290 Fax: (416) 440 0304.
BFO is a support group that runs information classes and provides social support for the bereaved. It is also able to put you in touch with affiliated societies throughout Canada.

Dying with Dignity. 188 Eglington Avenue East, Suite 706, Toronto, Ontario M4P 2X7. Tel: (416) 486 3998 Fax: (416) 489 9010.

This organization is a member of the World Federation of Right to Die Societies, and can offer information on euthansia, living wills, and legal matters relating to assisted suicide.

Widowed Support Group of Ottawa-Carleton. PO Box 16087, Station F Ottawa, ON K2C 3S9. Tel: (613) 723 0010. This group holds open monthly meetings at 7.30 in the evening on the third Wednesday of every month at the YM/YWCA, 180 Argyle Avenue.

Web sites

There is a huge number of Web sites on the Internet that deal with loss. Finding your way through the morass of largely subjective opinion isn't easy, but can be rewarding. There is a bewildering variety of perspectives on all aspects of death, dying and bereavement, as well as thousands of individuals' very personal accounts of how their life has changed because someone they loved has died. The quality is variable, but there are some very good sites that can also serve as links to the wider Net. Here are a few examples:

The Child's Loss
http://gladstone.uoregon.edu/~dvb/perrylos.htm
This is a series of notes by Bruce Perry intended as a set of guidelines for professional carers of children who have been bereaved. Despite the lack of cohesion, it's very accesssible for a general reader.

GriefNet
http://www.griefnet.demon.co.uk
GriefNet is the UK arm of Rivendell Resources which was started by Cendra Lynn in Ann Arbor in the USA in the early 1980s. The aim of the group is to provide resources on death, dying and relat-

ed issues. The HomePage is very user-friendly, and receives regular updates. It has well-ordered information for all interested individuals and professionals. There are also links to other Web sites.

Growth House
http://www.growthouse.org/
Growth House is a charitable trust based in San Francisco. Their award-winning site is well thought out and provides a human side to topics such as 'Grief' and 'Death with Dignity'.

London Association of Bereavement Services
http://www.swich.demon.co.uk/labs/links.html#top
LABS has a good list of links to resources for the bereaved. Particularly noteworthy is its list of sites for people of different cultural backgrounds and religions.

Men's Grief
http://bereavement.org/griefweb.htm
There is a handful of sites devoted to issues related to men's grief. This is one produced by the Bereavement Education Center, and deals with issues specifically related to men.

Michael Kearl's Home Page
http://www.trinity.edu/~mkearl/death.html
This site has interesting and objective information on homicide and suicide. The section dealing with the personal impact of death deals with the loss of a child, widowhood and grief. The list of links to other sites is good.

SIDS Network
http://sids-network.org/
This site not only deals with stillbirth and neonatal death, but also issues such as sibling grief. Most of the links are to other sites in the USA.

The Virtual Memorial Garden

http://www.catless.ncl.uk/vmg

The VMG is almost certainly the best of the many sites where you can place a memorial for your loved one. It's run by Lindsay Marshall of Newcastle University, and unlike many other pages, is guaranteed free of charge. There is an obituary page and links to other Internet memorial, and bereavement, resources.

WEBster: Death, dying and grief resources

http://www.katsden,com/death/index.htm/

This is probably *the* place to start your searches around the Net. This Web site comprises a comprehensive list of links to a host of pages on all aspects of death including philosophical and cultural perspectives, different approaches to care of the dying, the needs of the bereaved, practical matters, newsgroups and pages for health professionals.

Widow Net

http:/www.fortnet.org/WidowNet/

This is a resource for widows and widowers, and is based in the USA. The book list is good, particularly as it includes suggestions for reading from those who have been bereaved. There is an e-mail service which can get you in touch with others; you can expect about 60–100 notes a day. The section 'Dumb Remarks and Stupid Questions' is breathtaking in its range of the silly things that people say to those who have been bereaved.